This Way

More Better

Stories and Photos from Asia's Back Roads

By Karen J. Coates
Photos by Jerry Redfern

This Way More Better
Stories and Photos from Asia's Back Roads
By Karen J. Coates
Photos by Jerry Redfern

Edited by Janet Brown

Cover: Photo of Shu in Sapa, Vietnam, ©1999/Jerry Redfern

ThingsAsian Press
San Francisco, California USA
www.thingsasianpress.com

Printed in Hong Kong

ISBN-13: 978-1-934159-48-4
ISBN-10: 1-934159-48-4

Table of Contents

(A version of *The Plain of Jars* and *A Little Sip of Yunnan in Northern Thailand* first appeared in Travel + Leisure Southeast Asia.)

Introduction

I have traveled since I was seven years old. The journey began on the family room floor of a middle-class, midwestern home. There I sat on the green shag carpeting, with the pages of National Geographic spread before me: I want to go there and there and there. I want to write that and that and that.

And I did. I am lucky to have attained many of those childhood dreams. Much of what I wanted to see, I have seen. But now, decades later—as some of my own words appear in books that bear the National Geographic name—I realize that the value in my travels doesn't come from my own desires, but from other people's needs. For it is in honest conversations, when people open their hearts and minds and tell me about their lives, that I gain the most.

I grapple with the thought that I take a lot—an awful lot—from people who have nothing to give but their stories. And I, in return, have little to offer but the thought that their words will travel the world through my writings.

Sometimes people ask for things. For money, for gifts, for a better life to offer their children. Sometimes my husband, Jerry, and I offer little things—not because people ask, but because it would be the appropriate thing for any human to do. But usually, we try to tell the people we meet that we are not rich Americans laden with money. We are not an organization with a budget to help the needy. We are journalists, and the one consistent thing we have to offer is our word that we will spread their words—for people to see and read and learn.

That is why I travel now.

Each story in this collection has taught me something—about others, about the world, about myself. In this collection, my aim is not to preach the lessons I have gleaned or tell you what you should know. Instead, I hope to present these stories in such a way that you might find your own meaning in each encounter.

My former Gourmet editor, Bill Sertl, once wrote about why he prefers travels to vacations. "I like to come home smarter than I was before I left."

Books often offer a vacation from life. I hope, instead, this book takes you traveling.

A Note on Tone and Tempo

Many writers say they strive to achieve one consistent, distinctive "voice," something that tells the reader: This is me. And this is how I interpret the world.

There is a difference between voice and tone. If a writer is true to herself, her voice will be consistent. But her tone will vary with the stories she tells.

This book spans a dozen years through megacities and muddy jungles, happy times, sad times, times of love and death. It encompasses twelve years of growth within me, as a person and as a journalist. I have tried to keep a single voice that is true to myself, the observer and interpreter, and true to the people I write about. But each story sings a different song to a different tempo, depending on time, place, and circumstance.

A Balinese kite festival on the beach does not, will not, feel the same or sound the same as a Burmese dissident speaking of his tortured imprisonment. We as human beings change our tone when the mood of a conversation shifts. A single voice can speak to many beats. It is the same in nonfiction, and in storytelling that adheres to the truth.

Sapa, Vietnam

1. Shu's Story - 1999

She wears silver bangles in her ears and more around her wrist. She wears a hand-dyed indigo ensemble and leg warmers tied tightly with ribbon she stitched. Her name is Shu, she's ten years old, she's Hmong, and together we go walking.

Jerry and I meet her one evening as the sun droops over terraced hills, and twilight dims the cobbled streets of Sapa. It's a small burg in northern Vietnam, high on a skinny precipitous hill near the Chinese border. She finds us poking through the local market. She insists on friendship.

Shu makes music as she goes, carrying a portable cassette player in a black leather satchel. She pushes the buttons, and a friend sings in Hmong. She pushes them again, and a voice sings in Vietnamese. "That me," she says. She takes my hand, leads us through the darkening street and asks, "Tomorrow you leave?"

No.

"OK, tomorrow you go walking?"

Maybe.

"OK, tomorrow I find you." Then: "Here's a present for you."

She dangles a black ribbon embroidered with red and yellow flowers, green stems and leaves. Shu made it herself. She wraps it around my right wrist, ties it snugly, and tells Jerry he'll get one the next day. Then she swings my arm. She will find us, yes she will.

*****

And she does. The next morning, Shu pounces from the foggy market as we walk through town to an overlook above a cloudy abyss that leads to Cat Cat, a Hmong village in the opposite direction of her own.

"Hello. You remember me?"

Of course.

"Your name Karen?"

Yes.

She grabs my hand again and asks our plans. Where do we want to go?

Cat Cat, we say.

Shu will show us the way. And so we go walking, together, as she planned.

We follow the pebbly road and talk about Shu's business. She sells her mother's embroidered jackets, with little silver bell buttons. She sells the earrings, bracelets, and necklaces that her father carves and fashions. She stays in Sapa, two hours by foot from her village, Lao Chai. In town, she sleeps in a Vietnamese house with other Hmong girls who do the same. She walks home often, gives her parents the money she makes, then returns to Sapa to sell more trinkets. Shu has never seen the nearest city, twenty miles away. She's never been to Hanoi, never traveled beyond her walks. Her feet—brown, stained, cold in plastic sandals—they're her life.

And her life, at ten, mirrors the lives of many. It portends a life to come. They, the ethnic hilltribe women of Sapa, rap on restaurant windows and grab at foreign arms, hoping to sell their clothes and precious metals for a pittance to wide-eyed travelers who come here just to photograph them in their togs among their chiseled mountains. The girls start much younger than Shu. They continue well into wrinkled, grandmotherly life. Many ethnicities share the fertile nooks and crannies near Sapa, but the Hmong and Dao tribes govern the tourist trade.

But Shu—Shu is different. While others aim to conquer the traveler's wallet, whispering, "OK, OK, you buy from me," Shu works instead upon the heart. She bewitches with irresistible charm. She meets many foreign friends, takes them by the hand, and learns their native tongues. She opens her sack, retrieves a tiny purse, unwraps plastic from a parcel inside, and unravels paper around a stack of passport photos. There's Erik, John, Nancy, Margaret, and many more. From England, Holland, Norway, Australia. She pins the Canadian flag to her lapel. She dons a plastic flower in her headdress and carries a stuffed toy mouse, a gift "from Japan," she says. Shu sells, that's her job, the thing she knows, at ten years old.

No school today?

"Maybe I don't go to school and the teacher is very angry with me."

The teacher is in Lao Chai. English, tourists, money—they're all in Sapa.

⚔ ⚔ ⚔ ⚔ ⚔

After our walk, we offer Shu a full-fledged lunch inside the Four Seasons restaurant—a small local shop, not of the luxury chain—as Hmong and Dao women cluster around the doors outside. The proprietor grunts, preparing to evict our friend. We say it's OK, and the owner asks us again for assurance. She's our guide today, we tell the man. He chuckles.

Shu can't read the menu, English or Vietnamese, so we do the picking. We order green tea and fried rice with chicken. She gobbles intently, then clutches her belly and says she's full. Then she eats a spring roll.

It's time for business. Shu keeps her father's tiny carved hoop earrings pinned inside her jacket. Bigger items, such as shirts and necklaces, she stashes at "the Vietnamese house" on the edge of town. She leads us there, to a small structure of wood and earth smack against a hillside. Freshly dyed indigo dries out front. When the clouds part, the house snatches 180-degree views and a stellar look at Fansipan, Vietnam's highest mountain.

Shu takes us into the bedroom where five, six, then seven women assemble.

They say hello in chorus and dangle their wares before us. "You buy, you buy, OK?"

Shu riffles through a rice sack beneath a wooden bed and grabs a bundle, then leads us outside onto the stoop. She shows us two jackets with embroidered lapels and appliquéd squares with crosses and lines and triangles, all dyed deep, rich, and royal shades of blue. We look, touch, snuggle, admire while Shu takes a needle and thread to stitch a fraying seam. Women crowd around. They snicker at the handiwork, snorting that we should buy from them instead.

But we buy from Shu. We bargain a bit because it is protocol, and I feel criminal for taking so much and imparting so little. I am embarrassed how little we pay for two jackets and a bracelet. But she beams and thanks us profusely. Then she grabs my hand again, when the deal is done, and trots with us up the winding street.

"Me go with you."

We walk a bit. She hugs me, straddling my torso and clenching me in a warm embrace. "Thank you, thank you," Shu says.

We part with plans to meet the next morning. Shu will take us home to Mom and Dad.

*****

The next day, we go by foot, the way Shu does, down a bumpy road that slices across the mountainside. White rock looms above and a pit of air below, filling a valley wide and green. She holds my hand, then drops it to skip ahead at her own pace. Then she runs back to reunite with the two of us.

She points to buffalo and pigs and rice terraces. "You have?" she asks about our country. We answer sometimes yes, sometimes no, sometimes yes but different. Like the pigs. We watch black, hairy, snorting boars skirting narrow paths. We have pigs, I say, but pink and not so hairy. We have ducks just the same. We have streams tumbling down hillsides, wiping boulders clean. We do not have rice growing in geometry, row upon row upon square upon square, with water falling from one terrace to the next.

Shu doesn't know flat land. Hanoi? I tell her it's flat, like the road. No hills. She can't imagine it. "You no have?" she asks, sweeping her arms through the air, pointing to the postcard around us.

Well, not exactly.

I ask whether she knows airplanes in the sky, and she motions like a propeller. I tell her that's how we go from our country to hers.

"Maybe you have many, but me only one." In her ten years, Shu has seen just one airplane, a small one. It could never hold her whole village and more.

We buy cookies and three trunks of sugarcane at a shop where we turn from road to trail and begin our descent to the valley. The shop owner is Vietnamese. I ask Shu, when she buys food at the market, does she pay the same price as the Vietnamese? In reply, she asks what we pay for bread. There are foreign prices, Hmong prices, Vietnamese prices—in that descending order. "I pay more," she says. More than the Vietnamese. "I don't know why."

The subject recurs whenever we go walking. In her home—the Vietnamese. Later, over a snack—the Vietnamese. "I don't like Vietnamese," she says. And then she edits her words. "Sometimes friends."

But only sometimes.

*****

Shu leads us down, down through red earth that her neighbors plow and trample and chip away to carve new terraces, preparing for the next reap. She leads us up again, past children sloshing in the river, through a school whose blackboards show lessons in Vietnamese. This, she says, is the school she doesn't attend, the place where the teacher is angry with her for her absences.

Her home is farther uphill, through muddy trails and dried-up terraces. Twelve children scamper and chortle as we approach. Their noses drip, just like Shu's. Their skin is leathery, their hair snarly, their clothing ragged, their eyes runny. They devour the little goodies we bring.

Shu's home is like others nearby: dirt floor, wood frame, grass-and-shingle roof.

Hemp balls are stuck in the walls, and corn dangles from the ceiling. A blackened wok sits over a smoldering fire, and water trickles into a trough. There is one bedroom, beside the kitchen fire, with one bed and one big blanket. Light beams through cracks in the wall. Shu's aunt sits in the doorway with soft light illuminating an intricate pattern as she embroiders.

Shu's mother, Cu, chops pork fat with a cleaver. She goes outside to pick fresh greens with tiny yellow flowers, then returns to the kitchen and chops the vegetables on a thick wooden block. Shu stirs the fat in a pan while Cu adds the greens. Steam fills the room. Cu sets a small wooden table near the door. She ladles vegetable broth over cold rice, then fills our bowls with greens. All of us eat together while father Ga naps in the other room after taking a few swigs of his pipe.

After food, it's time for business. Shu's aunt displays her finished embroidery, a purse. There are silver necklaces, shorts, shirts, bags, rings, and bracelets—all for sale.

How much?

"You say," Shu replies.

She rarely names a price. We buy earrings and a blue-burgundy embroidered swatch for a tiny price that pleases Shu's family immensely. They give us a needlework square and batik shorts as gifts. Shu hands her mother the money we gave her the day before.

Tell your mother she does beautiful embroidery, I say.

"She knows, she knows, I tell already."

Tell your father he does beautiful jewelry.

"He knows, he knows. Yesterday, you buy bracelet." Our business is done, so Shu grabs my hand. "OK, we go to Sapa now."

And that's that. They all wish us well, and Cu tells us to return when we "have baby."

*****

We head back up from the hot valley, and sweat drips from Shu's brow. She unravels her leg warmers, then ties the hemp strips around her waist like a belt. We stop for Coke at a roadside shop. A European man we met the day before lumbers up the trail. Shu says she remembers him.

"I suppose you do," he says. He remembers Jerry and me. We saw him on the path between Cat Cat and another village called Sin Chai.

"Yesterday, you go Cat Cat," Shu says. "Me know you."

But the man doesn't recognize her. They all look the same to him, the Hmong girls wearing blue. There are so many, dressed alike, with dark brown skin and dark brown hair and dark brown eyes. But Shu remembers him well, and she knows enough to say so in English, Vietnamese, and Hmong.

"Cheeky," he says. "They're learning very quickly."

*****

She finds us again the next afternoon. The flap-flap of plastic sandals on asphalt ends in a robust hug. She's here, minus the fake flower on her hat, minus the hat itself, hair in pigtail braids. She has tiny, wispy bangs. She's the only Hmong girl we see without a traditional hat. Shu is Shu, and she does her own thing.

I donate photos to her collection, pictures of Jerry and me in Hue, the Imperial City. We tell her that's in Vietnam. "Oh, very good," she says and she gives us the thumbs-up.

She follows us as we move toward dinner. There is no electricity when we enter the Mimoza restaurant. Fluorescence and karaoke give way to candlelight. We sit near the window, and Shu tells Jerry to switch sides with her. She scrunches in the corner, wriggles in her chair. She can't sit still.

You have a problem?

"Yes. Police."

She's not supposed to be in the restaurant, and she doesn't want to be seen. Shall we move?

"Yes."

We move three tables away and our bodies conceal her. The electricity flickers on, and an old man in a beret smiles at Shu as he sits near the kitchen door, listening to a tape player croon the Godfather theme.

We order rice, tea, tomato soup, barbecue pork kabob, tofu, and fried vegetables. Shu inhales—four helpings, five helpings. She's ravenous.

Does Lao Chai have lights? I ask during another flicker.

"No, Lao Chai not have."

Did you eat today?

"No."

This the first time? No food yet?

"No food today."

Why not?

No answer.

No money?

She nods.

If you have no money, you don't eat?

She nods.

What do you eat at home?

"In Lao Chai, we have this and this," she points to the rice and the lettuce beneath the pork—but not the meat itself.

Same as we had in your house?

"Yes. Same same, what you had."

Rice, greens, pork fat. Every day?

"Yes."

You eat every day?

"Every day."

We clear the plates and she nibbles on peanuts, then settles into the large white plastic chair in a food coma. She smiles, twists her hair, loosens her leg wraps.

Does your Japanese friend take you to dinner?

"No."

Your Canadian friend?

"No."

Hmong women call to her through the window, and she goes briefly to check the matter.

We ask if she has a problem.

She nods yes. "Later...later with Dao and Hmong."

The Dao women enter as we finish. They drink tea and ask Shu something we can't understand. We can't begin to understand the complications of friendship between her, a ten-year-old Hmong girl in Vietnam, and us, two Western tourists who do more than buy trinkets.

We part and say good-night. We have seen the looks, the stares, at foreigners sharing time and food and love with her, a Hmong girl. She has "problem," as she says. But she is hungry.

*****

Life shuffles along, Jerry and I board
a plane, many months pass, and a
letter arrives.

"Hello Karen, How are you today?"
It's written in neat, careful penman-
ship. "Today where are you going?
Today I went for a walk with my
friends. Will you come back to Sapa
to visit? I miss you, do you miss me?
Do you remember when you came
to my village. I remember. I have the
photo that you gave me. Thank you.
You bought 2 jackets from me, I will
remember you. Never forget me, I'll
never forget you...I have a present
for you."

Enclosed are two bright, braided
bracelets.

Her name is Shu, she's older now.
She's Hmong, and she hugs my heart.
And every day, in my mind, together
we go walking.

A young Hmong girl named Shu in Sapa,
Vietnam. She takes tourists on walking trips
around the area and sells her mother and father's
handiwork to support her family.

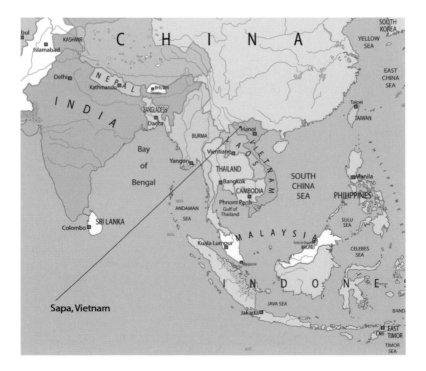

Sapa, Vietnam

2. This Way More Better - 1999

Two brawny little men in plastic sandals slosh through an icy stream, hurdling pools between slick boulders. They never miss a stride. They wear hand-stitched, hand-dyed indigo suits with shorts cuffed above sturdy knees and braided muscles. The men are linked by a bamboo pole, which rests upon their shoulders. From that pole hangs a hunk of hardwood, hacked into a solid block that weighs roughly a hundred pounds. The scent of sandalwood lingers in their wake. By the time the air clears, the men are down the hill and gone.

This is a scene that Jerry and I see again and again, sinewy men schlepping slabs of lumber through these vertiginous hills. They are Hmong farmers who live near the tiny town of Sapa, in the northernmost reaches of Vietnam. It's a hard life on society's fringe. The Hmong sided with the United States during the "American War," as it is called in Vietnam, and they still suffer the consequences. They are among the poorest villagers in Vietnam, often living far from schools and hospitals, roads and jobs. Food is often scarce, money even more so.

When not planting or cultivating their fields, the farmers leave their terraced villages on foot, searching for alternatives—namely the region's last ancient trees in the sandalwood family. Deep inside the forest, they find giants forty or more feet tall, six feet wide. They log the trees entirely with hand tools. They tote the wood by the strength of their backs and shoulders as they scramble up steep dirt paths, over rocky slopes, through muddy ravines. It takes hours, sometimes days, to lug a log from the forest to Sapa. On such journeys, the men carry a bag of cold rice which they freshen with a rinse in a stream—and that's it. That's lunch. Nothing more. In a couple of hours, these men conquer terrain that takes me—with a lesser load—a full day. They walk the wood to Sapa, and from there most of it travels to China, twenty miles away, via jeep or motorbike along a precipitous road high above streams, valleys, homes.

This is how Vietnam's last aromatic old-growth trees disappear, one by one, illegally. This is also how Hmong farmers earn enough money to eat, and perhaps buy a motorbike for their families. It's how adolescent boys earn money for marriage; how adults earn a little cash for drinking and gambling.

I remember the first time Jerry and I see a couple of loggers, fresh from the forests entering a village near Sapa. "They cut in the forest very far from here and bring to sell to China," says Hong, our guide who is leading us to a hilltribe wedding that day. A few moments later, we pass a clump of men squatting and gambling on the path, flicking wads of money into the dirt. Each 10,000-dong note is worth less than a dollar. Still, "that is a lot of money," Hong says. "A couple of years ago, some families only had maybe 40,000 dong." The extra money comes from sandalwood. Each man can earn 10,000 dong a day if he is willing to transport wood. "That's very good money for here."

Each wood slab sells for $20, $50, or $100 in Sapa—depending on who is counting and who is relaying the information. Here in these hills, numbers shift like the wind. But the visible truth is this: Wood fires the village economy. The people can make more money cutting logs than they do growing rice. And it changes things. For better and worse, it alters Hmong culture just as it refashions the landscape.

We walk with Hong beside a pebble-strewn river in the bottom of a valley. She points to the hills. "Once I took tourists into the forest on the other side of the hill. They asked me, and I said I think maybe the forest will be gone in ten years. Then the next year I go back, and it's gone already."

The forests are vanishing fast. The land changes in three quick stages—first cleared of big trees for sale at top price, then scoured for firewood and scraps, then burned and turned into paddies. "I know," Hong says, "I talk with some people and they say it's very bad." But villagers tell her if they don't cut the wood, someone else will. Twenty years earlier, a person could walk straight from Sapa into the forest. When we visit, it takes a day, sometimes longer.

*****

Jerry and I want to see it. Having lived in Oregon's timberlands, we want to see how old-growth grows in Vietnam; how the men cut it, trim it, and haul it out. We ask Hong if tourists go that far into the hills. She chuckles. "No, no."

But we persist. Locals tell us we have a quirky idea that requires the help of our guesthouse owner, who is accustomed to arranging unusual treks. He gives us the most rugged guide he knows, a twenty-two-year-old man I will call Duc.

A few mornings later, Duc arrives at our guesthouse late, harried and out of sorts. It's after nine, and we must go before we lose too much time. Jerry, Duc, and I pile onto motorbikes and ride into a thick mist shrouding a skinny road with a vertical drop to the side. Too fast, way too fast. My hands blister from gripping the seat, trying not to fall backward under the weight of my backpack.

The trailhead begins at a Hmong village called Ta Van. We cross a bouncy swinging bridge, pass a few homes, then head into a steep incline of red earth, glinting in an emerging sun. The trail goes up. And up. And up. No switchbacks, just straight up, plowing through the natural twists and turns of the hillside. Why make switchbacks? Duc tells us that would only add distance to the trip— no one wants more distance. "This is more better."

Duc is all about practicality—though we quickly learn that his differs from our own. He carries a Camel cigarette brand daypack full of supplies and rations: onions, spinach, potatoes, cabbage, chicken bouillon, two cooking pots, three bowls—though not a single change of clothes, nor eating utensils, nor a set of matches. He wears blue canvas shoes with a tiny tread. "I think these are very good," he says. "Five dollars. Cheap. I think those are very expensive," he says pointing to Jerry's hundred-dollar waterproof Vasque hiking boots. They do not impress him.

Duc scampers ahead to a crook in the slope. We rest. Already I have an amazing blister. Duc lights a cigarette (with an old lighter that will not last the day) and tells me the trek up Fansipan, Vietnam's highest peak at 10,312 feet, is tougher than this. "It's more steeper. Only up and down." He's climbed it fifty-nine times.

As we resume our ascent, we pass a group of Hmong villagers coming down. Two men break for lunch, wetting their small bags of cold rice in a fast-flowing stream. They tell Duc their log will sell for a hundred dollars in Sapa, and they intend to spend that money on food in the market. Eight or ten kids to a family is usual, they say. The money helps.

We continue, hiking over a stretch of rocks that bear odd scrapes and scratches. Duc says these scars are what remain of a 1979 Chinese military attack on Vietnam. The twenty-nine-day incursion covered terrain the Chinese didn't know, and they met the Vietnam People's Army, which had recently fought the U.S. to a standstill. The Chinese were mauled.

We reach San Mi Ti, an insulated village set in a pretty valley. A group of kids approaches us, fascinated by our every move. They are not healthy—snorting, coughing, sneezing, and scratching. Their skin is gray and cracked from a short lifetime in sun and mud, heat and cold.

Past the village, we enter a slash-and-burn zone where the air is choked with smoke and the rust-colored hills are denuded and smoldering. These are rice terraces in the making. In another year or two, this land will produce rice and vegetables, and the forest will exist only in memory. Men and women work the land, hitting their hoes against rock in a rhythm that creates a steady song. Chip-chip. Chip-chip. This is where we shall camp, near a wooden hut in a flat spot on the ashy hillside.

Duc has many ideas of propriety and he expresses them in proclamations. Eating dinner right now, as soon as the meal is cooked, is "more better" than bathing in a nearby stream or attending to raw blisters. Sipping tea immediately after the meal is "more better" than allowing our food to settle. And sleeping right here in a pasture atop cow dung is "more better" than searching farther up the trail for a more hygienic spot. He's surprisingly quiet about his now-dead lighter and lack of matches.

*****

Day Two starts with thick fog and a bridge: three bamboo trunks spanning rocky falls far below. Duc says the bridge is "more better" than anything else. Jerry and I wobble up the steps, clinging to the railing, trying to keep our heavy boots from rolling off the poles and sliding into the river. I don't like this route.

"Let me carry your pack," Duc says. "I think it is more better for you."

Perhaps, but my pride disagrees. Slowly, I cross. Twenty meters up the trail we meet a shallow stretch in the stream; we easily could have avoided the rickety bridge.

And so the trek continues. We crawl beneath a fence, along a narrow path meandering through a buffalo field, past a bin of excrement, and on to another rickety crossing on the same stream. There are trails on both sides of the river-bank. We plead Duc to choose one that sticks to a single side, avoiding shaky bridges.

"There is only one way," he says. And that is back and forth and back and forth and back and forth. "Everyone goes this way. I am sure." Right on cue, two men with a massive sandalwood log glide past us   straight down the middle of the stream, as though walking on a sidewalk.

So we cross the river again. And again. And again. We protest, to no avail.

"This is the last one," Duc says of the fifth crossing.

An old, wrinkled Hmong woman with indigo-stained skin watches with interest from a nearby rock. She offers to carry my pack. I smile but decline. Duc hears our exchange and says it's "more better" for him to carry the bag. Beneath my breath, I curse.

On the other side, we tramp through fertilized paddies. The earth is rich with sludge, my feet full of goo, my heel smudged with filth, a blister red and raw.

*****

We meet two kids on the trail. "They know where many people work in the forest," Duc says abruptly. "They will take us."

The trail turns into a red gulch that obviously roils with rainwater when the monsoons come. Duc goes ahead, out of sight, as Jerry and I squeeze between the mossy walls, sliding on wet leaves and mud-packed steps, twisting and turning among shady trees. When we reach the hilltop, we find Duc and the kids laughing and lounging. "We talking about getting married," Duc says, nodding at the kids, ten and twelve years old. He eyes the elder boy. "He says when he goes to cut the trees, he can get married. But now he cannot. No money, no honey!" Duc laughs.

A Vietnamese trekking guide known as Uoc Duc pulls a sliver from his finger while sitting on scrap wood at an illegal logging site in the jungles of Northern Vietnam near Sapa.

2. This Way More Better - 1999

We follow the boys to a young forest, far less magnificent than the sandalwood we seek. There is no sign of loggers, so we soon stop for the day and camp in a cloud. Dampness settles in our pores. The water doesn't sprinkle; it simply is, hanging in the air.

I bathe in a stream downhill, removing my shirt and bending to the water, rejoicing in the thought of clean skin. Suddenly, two boys emerge from the foggy nothingness around me. Where in the world did they come from? They look without staring, without any expression of wonder. They just look: There I am, there they are, here we are together, going about our business. They are dark, their bodies blue from indigo clothing. I cover my chest, and they continue on in silence through the trees.

*****

Later that evening, Jerry returns to camp after a solo exploratory walk and says he has found the trees—the big ones—ten minutes by foot over the worst terrain yet. But he has found signs of recent logging. Duc is skeptical—what would a foreigner know about logging?—but we make plans to go together in the morning.

The forest sings that night. It croaks and howls and sighs. All evening and deep into the darkness, frogs emit strange, deep-throated gurgles. Birds cackle, crickets chirp, monkeys hoot. And something metal clinks.

The next morning, I meet again the two boys who saw me by the stream. They carry a log down the mountain. Jerry, Duc, and I head in the opposite direction, searching for their work spot.

The forest changes abruptly, turning taller, deeper, thicker in an instant. Suddenly, sandalwood towers like redwood, higher than we can see. Old chisel marks mar some of the standing trees. Tiny game-size trails lead into dense, thorny shrubs. "Those are logging trails," Duc says.

Jerry takes us to a worksite he found the previous day. We tread over fallen trunks—trash that the loggers have left behind to rot. We find clearings where sawdust and wood chips litter the floor. We find a metal strap used for toting wood; it was left on the ground and now rust taints it after a night in the waterlogged air. Strangely, Duc looks around and dismisses this spot. He says no one has worked here recently.

A log six feet in diameter sits on the ground; another fallen tree lies split, baring its insides of bright yellow and orange. It smells delicious and would fetch thousands of dollars in the United States. But Duc says these logs are worthless. They are not perfectly straight and perfectly smooth, so the Chinese won't buy them. Then:

Tap, tap, tap.

"Shh," Duc warns. Loggers. "When they hear you, they will run away." He creeps ahead.

We wait a few moments, then follow to find him chatting with two tiny Hmong teenagers who look like boys, so small for their fifteen and seventeen years. They carry a handmade axe. They say little, and Duc directs us not to talk. "They think maybe we are from the government."

I try to ask questions, but Duc shushes me again. I ignore that and ask him to explain that we come from a place where logging is very different; people back home would want to know how the Hmong work here. Duc says nothing to the kids, but plays with their axe, trying to build rapport. The boys stand still like deer trapped in headlights.

Two young men join the scene, and we follow the four of them to a little log shop, a makeshift mill of sorts. The boys fasten together a two-person saw, which breaks under tension, sending a piece of the handle flying into Duc's head. Everyone laughs uproariously, and the air finally lightens a little.

Jerry tries to ask names.

Duc translates, then returns with the loggers' reply. "That is not such a nice question."

We ask Duc whether he's told the group why we are here and what we want to know.

"Yes, I've told them, but that doesn't matter," he says, annoyed. "They always think we are from the government. They don't believe." This is a strange remark, considering we look distinctly foreign, with blond hair and blue eyes; neither one of us has ever been mistaken for a cop.

It is illegal to cut sandalwood, but normally, the jungle hides the work. Few authorities venture this far from the road—too lazy, Duc says. We ask him what happens to the loggers who are caught. "Oh something very bad happens to them," he says. "Prison." We ask whether bribes can settle such matters, and he glances at us, surprised. "Oh! How do you know that?"

The whole while, Duc sits on a tree trunk whittling a wooden gun as the teenagers restart their work. They cut a little divot into a log, fill it with water stored in a hollow segment of bamboo, add a dollop of black acid from a crushed battery, roll a length of hemp string through the black mixture, then use the string to mark lines on the wood where they intend to cut it. Then they hoist the log onto crossbeams that hold it in place while they saw. The boys sit opposite each other with the log between them, slicing back and forth, back and forth. It takes two minutes to cut two inches into the wood. They are silent the whole time.

"Hmm," Duc sighs. "They think maybe I'm with the government," he repeats. And then Duc's story tumbles forth.

"Two years ago when I was guide only three months, I go with police to catch people cutting wood," he tells us. "And I go very fast. Police go very slowly… when I do that, sometimes police get angry with me because we make camp and I go up there," he points to the hills. "I make friendly with people and I say, 'Police down there. Don't go down there.'"

The kids suspect he's a government snitch. That's why they flinch at his questions.

Three years before that, Duc was a log smuggler. At seventeen, he and his twenty-four-year-old brother ran logs from Sapa to the Chinese border. They bought the wood from Hmong loggers, back when the trees stood much nearer to town. They transported them by road at night, when police were long asleep. It's all downhill from Sapa to the border crossing at Lao Cai; the highway winds around blind curves with vicious drop-offs to rocks far below. Duc and his brother tied the logs to the back of a motorbike and raced the route.

It was 4 a.m. when the moto hit a bad spot on a bridge. The logs scattered. The brothers sailed to a boulder field eighteen meters below. Duc broke his jaw, wrenched his arm, and scathed his cheek. He spent a month in a Hanoi hospital and lived. His brother did not.

"Now I don't do that anymore," he says. "Finished." But the police made Duc their tracker for a while. Caught red-handed, he couldn't refuse a new job as a government informant.

For several moments, the forest is silent, save for the shzzz shzzz shzzz rhythm of a saw. We watch the boys a little longer, then start our trek back to Sapa.

*****

The return journey is worse. Jerry and I slide and dive and tumble on our rumps through mud and rock and bamboo forest. We cling to trees that creak and moan as the wind channels through them. They seem to sigh and laugh as we grip their shiny bark and baby-step our way down a vertical descent. Jerry slips and his pants are covered in mud. "Be careful," Duc hollers unhelpfully from far ahead. For most of this trip, Duc has kept enough distance that he can't hear our grumbling. We realize he's seeking the safest routes for himself, avoiding contact with people.

But there must be an easier way, a better trail, I think. Still, Duc assures us this is the only way to go. "They use this trail to carry logs."

We know. Though we're not exactly wimpy, we have been passed by human beings who possess the strength of an ox, the agility of a cheetah, and the grip of a mountain goat. But we are not them.

Finally out of the forest, along the last stretch of paddies, Jerry slips knee-deep into a slimy slough of rainwater and buffalo dung. He swears, loud and clear.

Duc, far ahead as usual, turns and smiles.

"This way more better!"

A pair of Hmong boys cuts a sandalwood log into pieces small enough to be carried out of the jungle by Hmong men. Behind them is the jungle from which the log came. Much of the wood on the ground is scrap that will be left behind to rot. Even when cut into pieces and taken out of the forest, just a small portion of the sandal-wood tree is actually used. Logging is illegal in the Hoang Lien Son Nature Reserve, but a slab of rare sandalwood can fetch $20-$100, as much as a Hmong family can make in a year of rice farming.

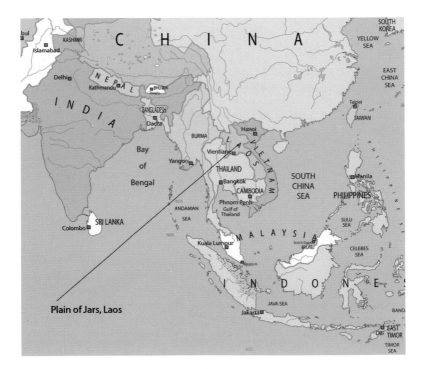

Plain of Jars, Laos

3. The Plain of Jars – 1998, 2005, 2010

Our introduction to the jars begins in the back of an old black Russian sedan as it careens across the mud-slick tracks of northeastern Laos. It's the middle of monsoon season, and a heavy one at that. The rain comes down, the mud comes up, and we can't see a thing through the spattered windows. After more than an hour of slip-and-slide through the countryside, we park in a gaping puddle. Our guide, a young man named Bounnyot, leads us up a steep path to a vista overlooking green peaks and valleys, and dozens upon dozens of enormous stone vessels. He could comfortably stand up in some of them and be completely hidden. The jars march straight across our line of sight. I have read about these archaeological mysteries; I expect wonder and awe. But I find a scene much more magnificent than anything I have imagined.

Then Bounnyot tells me he learned from his grandfather that the jars were gigantic tuns, built to hold lao lao, the local mind-bending hooch. They're ginormous whiskey flasks, all drunk dry.

Really? Does Bounnyot believe that?

"No," he chuckles. "Well…maybe."

It's a familiar tale to Julie Van Den Bergh, an archaeologist who has spent several years working for UNESCO, preparing the Plain of Jars for World Heritage status. In fact, she tells me she hears this story all the time: an ancient king named Khun Cheung, victorious in battle, built these jars to hold his celebratory elixir. "I don't have a problem with lao lao," she says. But science tells her these jars had greater purpose as the funerary urns of an unknown ancient civilization.

So far she has counted some three thousand jars scattered across ninety sites in Xieng Khouang province. There might be more. They're huge, up to nine feet tall and weighing several tons. The majority are carved of sandstone or granite. Some are round, others angular. Most are between fifteen hundred and twenty-five hundred years old.

Van Den Bergh bases her thoughts on work by Madeleine Colani, a French archaeologist who was first to study the jars in the 1930s and gave the Plain its name. When Colani excavated, she found jars with beads and cremated human remains. She also found a cave with burned bones and ash. She surmised the cave served as a crematorium, the jars as mortuary vessels, and the fields on which they sit as ancient cemeteries. Colani speculated the sites rest at an important intersection of ancient trade routes stretching perhaps as far as India and Vietnam. "What is a big civilization like that doing here?" Van Den Bergh muses.

And where did it go?

No one really knows, and it's unlikely anyone will find out anytime soon. Certain things have changed drastically since Colani studied on this windswept terrain, making future research precarious at best. Between 1964 and 1973, in an offshoot of the Vietnam War, the United States military dumped more than two million tons of bombs across Laos. The Plain of Jars was hit particularly hard. For various reasons—human error, failure to arm, faulty parts—up to 30 percent of those bombs did not detonate on impact. Millions of explosives remain buried in the soil today, still volatile. And they have killed and maimed more than twenty thousand Laotians since the end of war.

The Plain of Jars is considered one of the world's most dangerous archaeological sites. "Before you can do anything, it has to be cleared," Van Den Bergh says. "There's no way around it."

By that, she means cleared of unexploded ordnance (UXO). So for the first time in her life, she works with a bomb clearance team. Van Den Bergh takes us to meet Stuart Broome, a bomb disposal expert then with the Mines Advisory Group (MAG), contracted to remove UXO from several jar areas. They begin with the three most frequently visited sites surrounding Phonsavanh, the provincial capital.

We watch Broome's team combing the land for explosives, angling their way up and down skinny lines of a grid delineated by rope. Bomb clearance is painstaking work involving a variety of metal detectors. Every speck of earth must be searched, every signal investigated slowly, by hand.

"When they found a 250-pound bomb at Site 2, they cordoned off the entire area and evacuated," Van Den Bergh says. I later learn of a new local legend that attributes the dud to divine intervention. The bomb didn't explode, villagers say, because it landed in a holy place beside a jar. Locals speak of a rich girl and a poor boy who fell in love long ago. The girl's parents were unhappy with her choice of mate, and they forbade her from seeing him. So she and the boy met at the spot now known as Site 2, and each wished for a jar to mark that spot, with a tree between the jars to keep the two in eternal embrace. And that is precisely where the big bomb fell—and why it didn't blow up—among those jars and the tree.

That bomb is now gone, thanks to MAG, as are 210 additional items of UXO found at seven jar sites now safely cleared for tourism. But that's a small drop in the big buckets of bombs dumped across the province. "One of the main problems here is that tourists come unaware of how dangerous Xieng Khouang is," Van Den Bergh says.

When Broome meets tourists, he advises them to stick to the main paths and roads. "Don't deviate." He says that a lot. But that is impossible advice for Van Den Bergh to heed. She has to crisscross the province, mapping jar sites, greeting locals, marching through fields and forests looking for jars, sitting for hours through village meetings held on hard wooden floors in homes on stilts. Mainly she tries to persuade villagers that the jars in their backyards are valuable—to science and tourism—and that people will come to see the jars. An influx of tourists would mean an influx of money. Locals like the sound of money.

One day, we accompany Van Den Bergh to a small village called Na Xaytong, a bone-shaking hour's drive from Phonsavanh, across land uncleared of bombs. The villagers welcome us to a feast of cabbage soup, boiled chicken, green papaya salad, fried innards in duck blood, and many rounds of lao lao. Village women sit in the kitchen, chopping and chatting, while the men share the excuse to drink whiskey and avoid a morning of farming in the sun.

An elder named Chan Mootee tells me the jars have healing powers, and that villagers would pour water from the jars over the heads of sick children. Many years before, he says, local monks rolled a jar to the local temple to use it as a water basin. Several villagers suddenly grew ill, so the monks were asked to return the jar to its original site. Health was restored to the community when the jar was returned to its home.

Another day, at a village called Ban Xiengdi, near Site 3, we have a long chat with an elder named Son Sanit. He tells us that much of the local knowledge about the jars has gone with the elders before him. "The older people who knew about this history, they have already died," he says. But, like Bounnyot, everyone he knows grew up hearing stories about the jars and lao lao. When a Lao person dies, he says, it's essential for the mourners to provide whiskey. "It's the main thing in a funeral ceremony," he says. "It's the main thing of any ceremony." It's almost a plausible story. People around Phonsavanh drink a lot of lao lao, given the chance.

He never heard any of the archaeological explanations for the big stone vessels in his village. "Dead people were placed in the jars," Van Den Bergh tells him. "Then they were collected and placed in the ground…excavations around the jars have revealed bones. Burials."

An elder named Then Phom My speaks up. "So you've found bones?"

Van Den Bergh says she hasn't, but Colani did. That's news to the group. Listening, Son Sanit says he "half and half" believed her stories—though, still, "our parents never mentioned graves." They only mentioned lao lao.

*****

I think about those conversations on subsequent trips to the jars. Jerry and I visit four times, several days or weeks at a stretch—they seem to pull us back. In April 2010, we trek to a distant jar site near a mountaintop Hmong village called Ban Pakeo, accessible only by foot. It's a steep, sticky three-hour climb through a spritzing rain and clouds that cling to the trees. I sweat like a demon, but I feel great. The jar site sits in a serene forest of singing cicadas and flittering birds. Everything is mossy and damp from the rain. Orchids and trees grow straight through the stone, slowly crumbling and eating away at centuries of history. The jars reveal little conservatories of life. It is just as I remember, but wetter now in the seasonal rains.

*****

We make our introductory trek to Ban Pakeo with Van Den Bergh and a mapping team in 2005. It's a sizzling day in the dry season, and we come from a direction that leads us first to the mountaintop, then through slash-and-burn fields and into the sudden thickness of forest. There, all around, are the giants we've come to see. The team immediately sets to work, marking jars and measuring their dimensions. But Van Den Bergh pauses a moment and says, unequivocally, "They're beautiful, aren't they?"

It's the one assessment of the jars no one ever doubts or denies.

On the next page: Plain of Jars. A group of jars is illuminated by moonlight and strobe in this long exposure under the nearly full moon at Site 2 of the Plain of Jars near Phonsavanh, Laos.

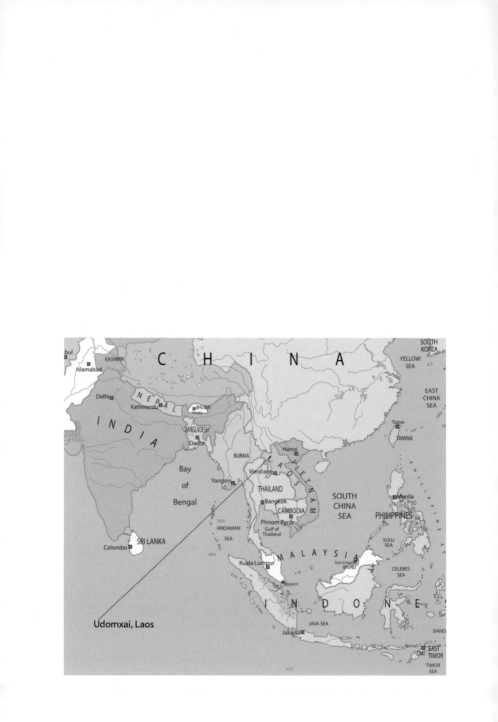

Udomxai, Laos

4. Getting to Sophoon - 2010

As we pass through the far north of Thailand, the landscape alternates between verdant rice and fields of ash. Smoke plumes swirl on the horizon and a gray film covers the sky. This time of year, farmers burn their fields in preparation for the next planting before the monsoons arrive. We cough and choke on the heavy air. But some paddies already glow with a fecund green. When we pass through those stretches of land, a familiar fetor slaps through the windows. It's the scent of ChemLawn, of chemicalized grasses and manicured yards. I am back in the Midwest among putting-green lawns with their little white signs that warn parents of recent sprayings—unsafe for children and dogs today! But here in Thailand, there are no white flags. Only odors.

We cross the big river in a small wooden boat, and the other side is the western edge of Laos. This is Day One of our long haul to Sophoon, a village way up high in Phongsali province on the road to Vietnam at the eastern reaches of the country. There, we'll meet Jim Harris, a retired Wisconsin school principal who dedicates his free time to clearing old American bombs from Laotian soil. During the war, between 1964 and 1973, the United States military pummeled this country with bombs. Up to 30 percent didn't explode, millions in all, and those old weapons remain embedded in the land. They are scattered far and wide across the country today. People still die. Nearly every day, a farmer or a child loses a leg or an arm or a life to a forty-year-old American bomb. Harris is the only American working on the ground to remove those bombs, one by one. We're going to see him at work, way up north. We expect it will take four days to reach him.

We arrive in Laos from Thailand just in time for dinner. The sleepy main drag of Huay Xai offers a little place with mulberry paper lamps and pretty pillows. It's a tourist-oriented restaurant, but the food is divine. The sticky rice is plentiful, good, and earthy. The orlam stew has tough old bits of cow but beautiful green chile and eggplant enhanced by the fresh flavor of dill. The jaeow reminds me of spaghetti sauce—but what a brilliant improvement: grilled tomato, chile, garlic, fresh cilantro, and oil. We eat, too, a plate of basic chicken laap—minty, oniony, pleasing.

After dinner, we visit the neighboring Internet shop—for the computers, not the toilet. A sign on the wall informs customers they are no longer welcome to "toilet service" in this store; please go to a hotel. Too many travelers before them have plugged the facilities here. Another notice out front asks customers not to request discounts, not to download improper items, not to smoke, and not to say "f**ck" or other impolite words.

We get little sleep that first night, in a big concrete guesthouse with thick wooden doors and rooms full of military men. They come and go, yammering and slamming through the night. Then soon enough, roosters start their synchrony of calls. The first crowing begins far away, but eventually, it is answered by one vociferous cock, right below our window.

*****

It's all day on a bumpy bus—hot and sticky, legs cramped, and body crunched into an untidy ball. Yet people are pleasant, and the Lao countryside slides past the window, showing us a tableau of rocky mountains. The hills stand like incisors—jagged, sharp, and mostly shaved of forest and fauna. Scarred by years of cutting and clearing for firewood and village development.

We arrive in Udomxai, just in time for dinner again. The town is a little slice of China, with all its plastic glory for sale in the local market, in a hodgepodge of dingy concrete cubbyholes. People come to Udomxai from all over the north of Laos to trade whatever they have, be it business or body or both.

We haul our dusty selves to a wooden shop that serves cold beer on a honking, busy street. This seems to be the place where minivans dump their tourists for an hour or two—a pit stop along the long stretch between Vietnam and somewhere else; somewhere not here, in Laos. The tourists order plate after plate of fried rice and bowl after bowl of ramen soup.

All the while we sip our beer, and eye a dim dangling light on the shopfront across the street. Lao people stop to eat. Lots of Lao people. The woman in charge keeps a big round basket of sticky rice displayed by the roadside. From fifty meters away, I can see an enticing row of greens lining the front of her stall. A small charcoal fire burns behind.

We pay for our beer and head for the dangling yellow light, where the woman serves us delicious noodles with a delicious dollop of meat paste and a delicious tray of lettuce and herbs, including a variety I have not seen (whose name I never learn)—mild, snaking sprigs with curlicued tendrils and leaves like hands. Mint, too. And lime. We order tam makhung, Lao papaya salad with tomato, sliced eggplant, peanut, and chile with building heat. The whole mess is the color of a summer plum, thanks to the addition of tamarind.

When our proprietor sees we like chiles—a lot—she brings us a clump and sets them on the herb tray. She instructs us to dip a chile into shrimp paste, stick it in the soup, and eat it whole. Delicious! She is right.

Next she presents us with something I have never tasted on its own—a small, brownish-purple stone fruit, which she calls maak kowr. I've seen it in the markets but its tart taste is unfamiliar to me. It puckers the mouth and sucks it completely dry. Dipped in salt and scooped up with a wad of sticky rice—yum.

On the return walk to our hotel, we stop at a Chinese Internet shop with a constant stream of women flowing through, presumably, to call families back home. They scream into the computers with shrill voices that drown all other noise. One woman catches a bit of phlegm in her throat, twists her head ever so slightly, and forcefully spits that loogie onto the floor.

*****

It's a Chinese road that leads out of Udomxai, a highway in the works. We pass Lao and Chinese workers all the way here, all men, breaking rocks by hand, all through the miles and miles of single-lane dangers with so many trucks and vans and blind corners on that narrow course.

The drive out of Udomxai snakes along a river that cuts through sharp mountains, mostly denuded, scraped of trees, covered in scrub and bamboo and the occasional field. But beautiful, still; the water looks turquoise gray, like a glacial stream. The road makes me think of my childhood cat, Snowflake, and the game we used to play: I'd trail a string, weaving through all the rooms of the house, slowly winding it in for her to pounce upon, as though attacking prey.

The road is that string.

We arrive in Muang Khua, then board a 5,000-kip (55-cent) truck to the river. There, a barge growls its way back and forth, pushed by a smog-spewing beast, the whole contraption attached to pulleys on a cable strung from hillside to hillside. Vehicles pay 100,000 kip to cross, but pedestrians pay nothing.

The afternoon idles as we await the next bus heading toward Sophoon. We have no idea when it will come. People tell us perhaps three hours from now, or perhaps 3 p.m. There is construction between here and the border, the road is closed to traffic through most of the day, and the bus we await must first come through the construction before unloading, turning around, and heading back. But we don't know when or how long that will take, and neither does anyone else—not precisely.

*****

Eventually on that bus during the afternoon's final hours, we enter the Sahara. Or maybe it's a flour factory—yes, that's it. We head straight into a world of billowing sand and dust. We become that world. We are miniature, driving through a giant mixing bowl as a pastry chef dumps colossal cup after colossal cup of pink-orange flour into the mess. It swirls, and we drive right through it fast on the bumper of the truck in front of us. Visibility is six feet at most. This is the road connecting Udomxai to Dien Bien Phu in Vietnam, under Chinese construction. They've carved giant walls into the mountains, eight stories high.

When we board the bus, the ticket seller tells us, "In three years superhighway." And he is right. The question is, Why? A new road in Asia almost always means the origin has something deeply desired in the destination. These hills are already logged. Is there gold? Oil? Coal? Asian roads aren't made for people. They're made for trucks. Follow a new road in a small Asian country, and you'll find the key to a more powerful country's heart.

But right now, it's a flour factory. And we drive right through it, bumper to bumper until the light disappears and we reach Muang Mai.

*****

Morning begins at six, in a new cloud—this one of water vapor—that drapes across the valley. I down a quick, hot glass of instant coffee and race across the bouncy footbridge to the local market, where a bus sits idle and empty. The only man inside works for the bus company. He tells me this is the bus to Vietnam. Our bus. The one and only bus today that will stop in Sophoon. When do we go? I ask.

"Right now!" he yells with a hustle to his voice.

OK, OK! I ask him for ten extra minutes so I can gather a few supplies at the market—which is the epitome of cliché, the ultimate "colorful market" with so many hilltribe women in indigo attire and vibrant embroideries adorning their hats and sashes and leg warmers; and each woman selling her own little piles of lettuce, scallions, cilantro, edible flowers, grilled fish, and banana-leaf packets of surprise. But I have no time.

I aim for the Thai/Chinese section where I find, among all manner of synthetics, two cotton mattress pads, four rolls of toilet paper, and soap. These are precisely the items we need for our encampment in Sophoon. We'll be spending our nights beneath mosquito nets on slat beds in an extra room at the village dispensary. We know the routine. We also know what to expect of the bathroom: squat toilet and a trough of cold water with a bucket for showering.

By the time I again pass the market women in all their colorful getups, the bus is gone. It's on its way down the hill, sloshing through the river and toward the guesthouse where Jerry awaits my return. I run with my arms and backpack loaded with mattress pads and TP. I bounce across the footbridge, past women making doughnuts and soup on the roadside. The bus is way ahead, beyond the guesthouse, and up the road by the time I reach Jerry in the doorway with the rest of our bags strapped across his back and hanging from both hands.

The guesthouse manager comes to our rescue. He loads our luggage onto his moto and drives it up to the bus. We shuffle behind, past more doughnuts and soups and tasty-looking mangoes for sale. It's only eleven kilometers to

Sophoon, but we've been warned: this is our only chance to get there today.

*****

So here we are. We've hurried up—and now we wait. We are about five kilometers down the road between Muang Mai and Sophoon, stopped—again—in a cloud in the forest. The Vietnamese-speaking hilltribe women at the front of the bus crinkle through plastic bags of food. I can't see what, but something smells wonderfully garlicky. All I have is a bag of dried riverweed with sesame, purchased at a midpoint stop between Udomxai and Muang Khua the other day. Yesterday? I'm already losing track of times and towns and segments of this journey-to-begin-our-journey. I've lost count of dates; this happens in Laos.

Jerry returns to the bus after a short walk. He's found a sign: the road is closed daily for construction between 7 a.m. and 10 a.m. Right now, it's a few minutes past eight.

An hour passes. We both, separately, get out to investigate a big truck in the road ahead. Apparently, from the looks of the scene, the vehicle took the corner too fast and too sharply and stuck itself at an angle into the dirt that serves as a temporary road. The truck is—was—carrying sixteen concrete electrical poles and a load of rebar. Now it is wedged across a hairpin turn in the road like a fishbone stuck sideways in a throat. It must move before we or anybody else can; we hope that happens before 10 a.m. when the road reopens. Several men begin tying a cable to the truck's front end.

Meanwhile, another batch of men, both Vietnamese and Lao, spread banana leaves in a bramble patch beside the blocked curve. Lunchtime. They invite us to eat—a mound of rough golden sticky rice; beef cooked with chile, ginger, and greens; spicy jaeow dip with chile, garlic, fish paste, scallions, and the flavor of soybean. The food is salty and nourishing, and it stops the rumble in my empty stomach. The men do rounds of Red Bull mixed with Lao whiskey in a green bottle with a flowery label. They offer, but we politely decline.

The wedged truck's driver is lunching with us, and he says the accident happened either five hours ago, or around 5 a.m. Either way, it would be roughly the same: it's almost 10 a.m. now. He wrecked the truck, "then he slept," reports his friend, the Red Bull-whiskey instigator. Between swigs, he proudly shows us a cell phone photo of his eight-month-old daughter named Su-Su.

By now, a caravan of morning traffic has arrived behind the bus. It's a whole line of vehicles that lingered a few extra hours in Muang Mai. Those passengers, I'm sure, are fully tanked on Lao coffee and buffalo noodle soup; I'm certain they enjoyed leisurely breakfasts in the village. We, on the other hand, caught the 8 a.m. bus, which went three miles out of town and stopped.

A newly arrived truck and an SUV jockey for position at the front of the line. Both vehicles wriggle ahead of our bus, up near the little wooden blockade that keeps all this traffic at bay. Several villagers park their motos and wait. Several men and women and kids squat on the roadside, and wait. The fog burns off and the temperature rises. We wait.

It's after ten now.

We all wait.

Bus to Sophoon. A man naps in the front of a bus waiting for a road that is under construction to open in northern Phongsali Province. The road connects to Vietnam.

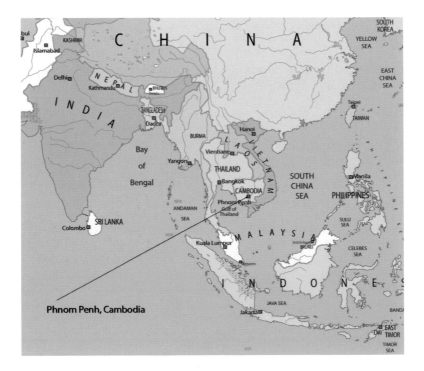

Phnom Penh, Cambodia

5. Picturing Cambodia – 1998, 1999, 2001

A single shaft of light pierces a shabby roof, landing upon a two-meter tray of bread in a sooty room. The kitchen is grimy and dim, except for that light and flames beneath that tray. Two skinny, sweaty men shuffle the bread, facing the inferno. I gaze at that photo, and I feel the heat.

The picture takes me to those men, making those little loaves of bread. I am there among them, average workers accustomed to hard days in a country of little payback. Theirs is a tedious job, of creating the bread that defines a Cambodian morning. Sold everywhere, on every street across Phnom Penh; dipped in coffee, drizzled with milk, sliced and crammed with meat. It all begins in that room, with the hands of those men, beneath that blazing shaft of light.

*****

I archive moments in photographs. There's something about pictures—they show facts, they evoke emotion. They reveal details forgotten in time—logos on shirts, holes in shoes, brown streaks on teeth exposed in smiles. I can write by hand, punch letters on keyboards; but sentences are two-dimensional, flat black on plain white. Pictures help me paint words in a way that conveys a story's intricate colors.

Jerry and I have work that runs in cadence. His images, my words—the combination builds the rhythm of a place, a time, a piece of life. Jerry, sitting in his office, types captions, calling my name and asking for a spelling or date. Later, stuck in midsentence, I turn to his stash of photos, a treasure of detail. So many tidbits in a picture, so much more than a notebook can hold. Writers can't possibly record all that a camera can see. A blackened fingernail, a loose thread, the camouflage pants of a father watching his baby die. Through photos, I can sense events in other ways; I can smell the jasmine, taste the mango, feel the scorch of a midday sun. I can hear horns on a busy street, or the chanting of monks at 4 a.m.

*****

It's 1998 when Jerry and I begin work in Cambodia, documenting a shredded society at the end of civil war. I go there for a newspaper job while he shoots freelance for a wire service. We leave a year later, but we return again and again, always guided by people and memories; always adding to our archive of times both beloved and bedeviled.

I decide to write a book about the country after war. I type beneath gray Oregon drizzle; I tinker beside a frozen lake in winter twilight. I write where I am, which is always changing: Bangkok, Bali, Dili, Milwaukee; then the sweltering streets of Cambodia all over again. We return for a month or two and we're instantly shaken alive. This country is an amalgam of loveliness and wretchedness, blended.

Our Khmer friends complain that tourists never see them, never see real Cambodians. Short-term visitors, they say, see everything framed by the Killing Fields and Angkor Wat: 1.7 million dead by genocide, the world's largest temple, thousands of skulls, carved angelic dancers; all couched in a "newfound peace" that brings economic reform. That's that, Cambodia in a nutshell. Somehow, 13 million people add up to a war and an ancient ruin.

A social worker tells me tourists doubt him when he says 70 percent of Cambodians wonder what they'll eat tomorrow, 25 percent fret about food next week, and only 5 percent never worry at all. The tourists he meets shake their heads in disbelief. They see no evidence of such things. "They just visit the happy places," he tells me. They tour the ancient temples and chat with countless smiling children. People appear content on the surface, but a hunger burns beneath.

I'm not writing a book of happy places. I'm writing an account of life. So I crouch on the carpet of an office floor, pawing through prints. I peer over Jerry's light table with a loupe around my neck. I pry paintings from our wall and I project slides, large as life, on the bare spots left behind. There, I scan the enlarged images for details I might otherwise miss.

*****

That first year we live in Phnom Penh, Pol Pot dies and the last Khmer Rouge soldiers defect to the government. We watch the war fade and the peace founder, and we learn that war and peace aren't necessarily distinct. They're colored by the in-between: the scarlet of spilled blood, the baby blue of protest banners, the green of an army enlisted to protect or kill, depending.

I see the pictures in color.

I see a ragged tarp staked to a garbage pile, a mountain with no visible bottom. I see thirty-year-old Mai stationed in this plot of filth. Flies pester her face; she ignores them. She has two kids and a husband—they all work at Stung Meanchey, Phnom Penh's infamous, ever-expanding dump.

Jerry and I hike through that cesspool, where two hundred families scavenge for a living. Switchback trails descend from trash that flows and tumbles ever closer to neighboring houses. The trucks come, one after another, with kids hanging from the rear, enjoying the ride. Women pick through a city's discarded plastic bags, salvaging bits for their dogs. Others sort through rotten food, saving anything their families can eat. A vendor sells ice slushies from red and blue baskets. A barefoot man clangs his bell, selling ice cream. Little yellow chicks peck at mounds of shredded denim. Dozens of workers rake through debris as fires burn all around.

The garbage goes and goes until it reaches calm lagoons and spinach planted in neighborhood gardens. Things converge on the fringe of that dump: it's a melding of cows and fields, homes and fishermen, life and grime. No one wants to be there. "It smells. I get sick, I get headaches and stomachaches, bad health," says a seventeen-year-old scavenger named Kut Vundy. He would rather be in school. He wants to become a teacher. But his parents don't work and scavenging is the only way he knows how to provide.

*****

I see another field, far away. A cow with a studded collar lies in a rice paddy, the ground crackled and dry. A blue sky and cottony clouds hang above a tall building packed with skulls. Eight thousand human skulls.

Men drive oxcarts in charming light, critters feed among human remains. At Choeung Ek, the Killing Fields, life persists around mass graves. Bones poke from paths circling pits; shirt scraps litter the ground. People come to search for bones and teeth—anything of a loved one long gone.

As the years pass, little changes occur in the ground. I return to find the dead prodding their way into present life. I find more bones, more shirts, more pants, two teeth. More dead people poking through the soil. Every year, the rain washes more dirt away; the weather bares more secrets. Little kids come to play kickball among the graves. One day, I find the crown of a skull newly exposed, but the rest of the head remains buried.

Just a few miles away, in a quiet neighborhood where the streets aren't paved, is Tuol Sleng. The name means a poisonous place on a mound, where the guilty are kept. It was a high school before 1975, a prison after. Fourteen thousand people or more were tortured at Tuol Sleng, then sent to Choeung Ek to die. When the Vietnamese invaded Phnom Penh in January 1979, they found dead and bloodied bodies still shackled to their beds. Just a handful of prisoners survived.

The Khmer Rouge kept meticulous records. They left hundreds of black-and-white photos of faces soon dead. I see little boys and girls who would have been my age today. Some of their eyes are overcome with fear. Others show no emotion at all, as though the human spirit already left their bodies, just three or four years old.

Deeper inside the museum, I see a map of Cambodia fashioned from hundreds of skulls. Eventually, that map is removed and many of the skulls are placed behind glass, displayed in cabinets. History gets put on a shelf.

But it's hard to look ahead when the past still trails so close behind. The wounds of genocide spread from generation to generation, manifesting in random violence, rampant poverty, social upheaval, and personal psychological traumas. Up to 40 percent of Cambodians suffer one or another form of mental illness. Khmers say the spirits of the dead are not at peace—neither are their descendants.

*****

I see five boys resting on a rock at the ancient Angkor temples. They huddle over Jerry's camera, exploring the gadget's possibilities. They are curious, smart, inquisitive. Many kids at Angkor don't regularly attend school, but they learn on the job. They lead foreigners through the corridors of Angkor history, making money, learning English, getting ahead. They speak two languages, sometimes three or four. Hard work and new lessons every day. At eight or ten years old, they determine the secret of success for Cambodians born without status or money: Do it yourself, because no one else will do it for you.

One little boy is named Hui. Dressed in a tattered yellow shirt, his only shirt, he stands at the edge of a murky pool among eight-hundred-year-old ruins. He plays in a field of four-leaf clovers, in an irony he will never understand. He twirls the stems between his fingers and palms.

Hui guides us through the temples, treating us to a sunset view of Angkor Wat from the perch of a small mountain (back before so many thousands of tourists discovered that spot). When we depart, he asks for 500 riel, about 13 cents, for his daily wage. Happy with his earnings, Hui scampers off with his friends. After a long day's work he allows himself to be a kid again.

*****

I see progress in another boy, a barefoot boy in a dark blue shirt with a left foot bound in bandages. His name is Cheth, he's eleven years old. He has no parents. And for a long time, he wanders the streets. The foot was crushed in an accident. It grows big and gangrenous, but Cheth refuses help. He listens to his friend who tells him a mangled foot will draw attention—and money from tourists.

I hear about Cheth from a colleague, and I go to meet him. I find him at a shelter for street kids, and there I see him in a different light—cleaned and fed, with a doctor who thinks his foot will heal. Cheth likes his new home, the regular meals, the friends he's made. His buddy stops by every now and then, trying to lure him back to the streets, but Cheth says no. He's made other plans now, for school and a future as a mechanic.

About twenty thousand kids roam Phnom Penh's streets—some orphaned, some simply sent to make money. Some go only when their families have nothing to eat or sell; others live on the pavement all the time. The poorest kids without homes are barefoot and dirty, with perpetually runny noses. They have scabs on their skin, already tough like worn leather. Their hands and toes may never scrub clean. They play and laugh and skip as children should. They collect coconuts and flowers from the leftovers of Buddhist temple offerings. They sleep on concrete. They wash and drink from the filthy river. Some take drugs, some sell their souls, some cut themselves with knives.

I see them all in pictures.

*****

I see the portrait of a fourteen-year-old girl. I never meet that girl; I know her only from Jerry's photos. She shrouds her face with a shabby checkered scarf. Her mother sold her to a pimp who stole her body, "her happiness," as Khmers often say. She escaped the brothel and found a safehouse full of other girls, bought and sold, with stories just like hers.

I have met other girls like that: girls who are scarred inside. Some feed their families through prostitution, some have no choice. Some are chained to bedposts and never let outside; others choose to stay because they have no idea where else to go. It's a dismal trade, in the seediest parts of town (and some of the nicest, too), attracting the most wretched of people (and some of the most upstanding, too). Brothel owners know the youngest kids—boys or girls—sell the best.

*****

I see the bleeding head of a trampled man. Eight frames, click click click, all in a row: the systematic details of a vigilante attack outside our apartment. A young man on a moto tries to snatch a woman's purse, and a crowd knocks him down. They chase him up the street and around the corner to the sidewalk of an Internet cafe, where he is caught. The mob kicks and shoves and pounds him to the ground. It's lunchtime; the sun is high. A boy we see every day selling papers stomps the man's head on the sidewalk. The gutter is wet from recent rain. Dozens of onlookers crowd around—mostly kids and men, wearing the tattered attire of life on the street: worn kramas, torn shirts, plastic flip-flops.

The crowd stops before the man dies—unlike some beatings. He sits for a moment, forehead clutched in the palm of his hand, then slowly stumbles to a shopfront where a dozen customers have gathered for a look. The shop owner gives him a pitcher of water. His shoe sits in the street around the corner where some cops congregate. Another officer already has ridden away with the man's moto.

*****

As I dig through boxes of slides and prints, as I examine images on CD, I find more questions than answers. What becomes of Hui and his clovers? Of Mai at the dump and Cheth with his foot? Of the thief without a shoe? I imagine their lives shuffle along—one step forward, another step back—as the years mosey on. But most of the strangers I encounter in chance events, I rarely see again. I know them only through memories, through words and pictures.

*****

I see pictures of hope, too. A man who de-mines his homeland by hand. Former Khmer Rouge soldiers protecting a near-extinct species of turtle. Monks caring for kids orphaned by AIDS. Pictured against a backdrop of despair, they are dazzling images.

One day, I am put in touch with an American woman who plans to adopt a Cambodian child. She wants to know about the country. Can I tell her a few things?

I write an essay. I start with the news. I give her statistics on health, mortality, sanitation. I assemble paragraphs on history tracing the ancient Angkor empire to the Vietnam War, to the Khmer Rouge, and to the country's politics today. But that's just background. A statistic has no depth; a date has no voice or breath. Just black-and-white words on paper, framing one interpretation.

So I return to the photos that show what she and I really want to see: emerald paddies, fattened silver fish. Little boys with shoeshine kits. Little girls that smell of sweat and dust from a life on the land. I tell her what I see, which leads me to how I feel.

And I am lost in the writing, back in Cambodia, with the photographs in my lap.

5. Picturing Cambodia - 1998, 1999, 2001

Left: Views from Choeung Ek, a Khmer Rouge killing field on the outskirts of the capital, Phnom Penh, preserved for history as it was found by invading Vietnamese troops in 1979. Human bones and skulls still protrude from the ground where perhaps 14,000 people were murdered and buried.

Next page: A child scavenges the water from inside a discarded coconut at a Hindu temple along the waterfront in Phnom Penh. Locals come to pray to the Hindu god associated with the temple and leave food as an offering.

Below: A baby hangs for the day in a net suspended from the ceiling at an orphanage in Siem Reap, Cambodia. The children are rarely let down, and their legs are stunted from not walking enough.

5. Picturing Cambodia - 1998, 1999, 2001

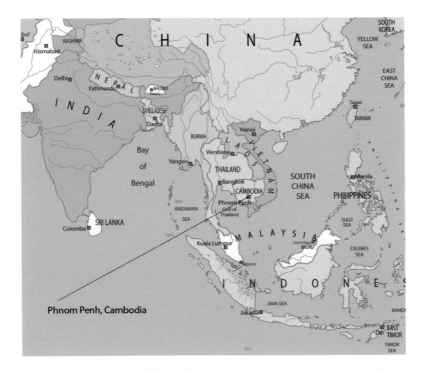

Phnom Penh, Cambodia

6. Running on Empty - 2003

When the early morning sun crests the outer wall of Phnom Penh's Old Olympic Stadium, Mok Bonthoeun is there inside, circling the cinder track in the patchy light. He finishes his five-kilometer warm-up, stretches, and changes into track spikes. The shoes—old and rusty with holes the width of his fingers—are a gift from the Cambodian government. He laces them with pride. And with that, he begins again fifteen times around the track—fast.

That's his plan, but the plan may change. He's tired now. "Maybe ten times." He ran three hours yesterday, and he's had nothing to eat this morning. "No money," he huffs. "I come here and hope to borrow money from my coach, but today he doesn't come."

People love Mok Bonthoeun. Teenaged girls hug the sidelines, chanting "Baby, baby!" as he breezes by. He could lead his nation in the Olympics one day. And yet, the country's best distance runner can't afford a 50-cent breakfast.

*****

I first meet Bonthoeun in Hun Sen Park, where I dodge packs of kite flyers and badminton players in an attempt at an evening run. I feel someone breathing down my neck. I turn my head and there he is, shiny red running togs drenched in sweat. "Hello!" he says. "I am a professional runner!" He is trim and muscular, and it is obvious he's telling the truth. We run a lap side by side, silently, with Bonthoeun pushing the pace. Then he starts talking.

He lives at home with his out-of-work parents and six younger siblings. He tries to support them, but he can't. "It is very difficult," he says. The government pays him, though he never knows how much he'll get. "They said $100 a month." He doesn't get that.

I ask if he has a phone number and he says no, he's too poor, but his coach has a number, which I memorize as we run. I tell him I'm a journalist, but I am not as great a runner as he, and by the third lap I'm ready to leave. So Bonthoeun stops beside a young man sitting on his motorcycle at the edge of the park and asks for pen and paper. His sweat drips all over the page as he writes his name, "marathon runner," and his coach's number. He hands me the page, apologizes for the sweat, smiles, and asks if I'll be back the next day.

*****

The next day, I meet Bonthoeun in the park again. He brings a copy of an application for a half marathon he might or might not be able to attend in Portugal, depending on whether the Cambodian government decides to send him.

He tells me he has no money, he can't afford the food it takes to fuel a winning runner. "I have nothing for my body." If he were an athlete in Vietnam or Thailand, he says, he would not have these problems. But Cambodia is different. "It's not like other countries."

Yet he keeps on running, somewhere between 65 and 115 miles a week, every week. He makes his own schedule. He trains twice a day, two hours each morning and one in the afternoon. When he's not circling that old cinder track or the city's central parks, he's doing his long runs, out of town, in the smoke-choked air amid cows and oxcarts, motorcycles and SUVs, dogs and bikes. It's mayhem.

*****

Bonthoeun invites me to his house. It's a long way from Hun Sen Park, over the Vietnam Bridge, down a dusty road, then a skinny dirt track to a four-room hut squeezed into a row of shacks. Inside, on one end of the family room, is a cabinet with four pairs of old, blown-out running shoes. On the other side is a gilt Buddha statue on an altar of flowery offerings. "I pray all the time," Bonthoeun says. "I believe in Buddha. I always pray before competitions." Bonthoeun's family keeps a stash of mementos, medals on ribbons and dusty trophies—evidence of his success. But the house is otherwise Spartan, just a simple wooden home with a metal roof and windows with shutters kept closed through daytime heat and open during cool, evening breezes.

Bonthoeun sits cross-legged on the hard floor, discussing his life and career and the state of Cambodia, with his mother nearby and his father smoking a cigarette in the doorway. He talks about money. The government paid Bonthoeun $600 the previous year. So far this year, he's received $30. "I have no other money," he says. "This is my life. This is my future."

Every day, he eats a little fish. "Sometimes I eat cheese with cucumber," he says. "Sometimes, during a month, I have beef only one time. Sometimes not at all because I have no money. For my energy, I eat fruit—but it depends on money, too." He eats the most of anyone in his family. "But I also think about my brothers and sisters, who are smaller than me, because they need food too."

He pulls out an old pair of Adidas Concerto running shoes, ripped and ragged. "Ten dollars secondhand," he says. They would have been eighty dollars new four years earlier. The shoes have carried him through two years of races.

He first raced in 1995, and by 1999 he won the silver medal at the Arafura Games in Darwin, Australia. He shows me photos from the Angkor Wat Half Marathon, which he runs every year—and wins. He has raced in Laos, Thailand, Singapore, Indonesia, Malaysia, Australia. "Mostly I go to Vietnam." He once placed tenth in a marathon there, and won thirty dollars. He ran his best half-marathon time, 1:15, in Saigon two years before. He ran his best marathon time, 3:06, in Singapore in 2002. The host country always pays his hotel rooms, meals, and airfare, but Bonthoeun earns little else to take home. "I am the best in Cambodia," he says, but "abroad, when I race, I can compete with the other runners only fifteen kilometers—then I feel weak."

Running isn't Bonthoeun's chosen career—but it is his salvation. "I want another job, but nobody can help me. I want to be good with computers and speaking English." But he never made it beyond secondary school. Bonthoeun started running ten years ago, mostly because he had nothing else to do. "I had no money, and also little knowledge, because I'm poor." At that time, civil war still simmered in the west. The Cambodian government quickly conscripted eighteen-year-old males to fight the Khmer Rouge. "It was very difficult to study because the government always arrested people to be soldiers," he says. National athletes with government coaches could avoid the draft. Bonthoeun didn't want to fight, so he ran.

He was born in 1975, the year the Khmer Rouge stormed into Phnom Penh and herded everyone to the countryside. In the following four years, at least 1.7 million Cambodians died of disease, torture, and starvation in a genocide the world learned about years later. The Vietnamese invaded in 1979 and stayed a decade. In 1993, the United Nations organized democratic elections in the biggest peacekeeping mission of its day. Meanwhile, Khmer Rouge rebels moved to the jungle, and civil war continued in the countryside until late 1998.

Bonthoeun's father, Mok Samoeun, joins the conversation. He tells me he spent the first two years of the Khmer Rouge regime in jail, and he lifts his pant legs to show the dark scars of shackles. Like most in Cambodia, this family has endured a lot. "I'm proud of my son," Samoeun says, "but I also suffer inside…he has no salary for feeding the family…he has fame but no money."

Bonthoeun chuckles. "If I were a runner abroad, maybe I would be a millionaire."

His father boasts: "In Australia, he got second place. He could have been number one, but he didn't want to be number one, because the winner was the Australian host who took him in and was very kind. He lost by one step."

Bonthoeun smiles and confirms the story. He didn't want to embarrass his friend.

I ask Bonthoeun to compare his country to the others where he has raced.

"Very different—the same as sky and earth. One is up here and the other is down there." Economically, Cambodia is at the bottom and every other country is above.

By now, Bonthoeun's little sister, Mok Chamrong, and his brother, Mok Mony, have gathered in the hot little room. Their pride gleams in their eyes. "I'd like to be like my brother and go abroad, run everywhere," Mony says.

Speed runs in the family, Saroeun says. "His uncle before was also a runner, too. But he died in the Pol Pot regime."

*****

Prum Bunyi sits behind a large desk in an office laden with sporting memorabilia. His name card lists half a dozen titles: deputy director of Physical Education and the Sports Department for the Ministry of Education, Youth and Sports; cabinet director of the Cambodian National Olympic Committee; secretary general of the Cambodian Sep Aktakraw Federation; deputy secretary general of the Cambodian Badminton and Petanque and Sport Boules federations; and national course director.

Prum Bunyi is a big man in Cambodia—but it's Bonthoeun who wins his regard. He says Bonthoeun is the country's pride and hope in the half marathon. He is the best runner since To Rithia, a national hero who ran in two Olympic marathons. To Rithia was one of five Khmer athletes to compete in Atlanta, the first games to which Cambodia sent a team in twenty-eight years. He made the nation proud. But To Rithia is retired now, and Bonthoeun is the next runner in sight.

Bunyi explains to me the stagnation of Cambodian sports. The country is still recovering from its past. Roads, schools, hospitals, courts, pagodas—they were all destroyed, and they haven't been fully restored. It will take a long time for Cambodian athletics to come back. "This is because of the war," Bunyi says. "Before the war we were very strong, and after the war we are very weak."

When he was a child, Bunyi played volleyball and basketball. "I was the best athlete in the school." Sports were well loved at the time, and Cambodia had top-level football and volleyball teams. Kids moved from the countryside to train at a national sports center in Phnom Penh. But now, "we do not have an adequate way for them to train."

Bunyi is an optimistic, congenial man in a pressed white shirt. He has an aura of professional grace. If anyone can bring Cambodian sports to international light, Bunyi gives the impression he can. "I just hope that by the support from the government and private sector, we will stabilize our situation and recover very soon…we need a good thing in the future."

But the government alone cannot and will not fund Cambodian sports. Athletes need sponsors, and the Sports Ministry appeals to overseas coaches for help in training. The ministry snatched a five-year, $1 million grant from FIFA to develop Cambodian football, and many countries hope Cambodia will one day host regional sporting events. But skills are lacking. Even if the country builds the stadiums, hires the coaches, sells the tickets, and puts on a good show, Bunyi says, Cambodia still lacks athletes.

"As a host, we must win to make our people proud. If we are the host and we get nothing, how do we respond to the people?"

So Bunyi is pulling the best competitors from each province, building a national Olympic Team "step-by-step," the favorite phrase across this country of piecemeal development. And maybe, someday, Cambodia again will rank among the winners. "We just try. We will try our best."

*****

Meanwhile, Bonthoeun's stomach is growling and his mouth is hissing. He says a word in Khmer and searches for the English translation: corruption. Ubiquitous in Cambodia, the United Nations calls it one of "four basic evils" plaguing the country. Its siblings are poverty, violence, and lawlessness. He has much to say about this issue, but he asks me not to print his words because he is afraid. In general, he says, "I'm disappointed." He thinks too many people in Cambodia care little about sports "because they only think about power."

Sometimes he wants to quit, but he has no idea what else to do. "In this sport, the runner tries very hard, but the runner is not rich…the runner becomes poorer and poorer." He has an old Khmer adage for this: "We plant a farm, but we reap no harvest."

Bonthoeun determines most of his training schedule himself. He does not have the benefit of a nutritionist, a personal trainer, or a library of running literature. His schedule is scrawled in a shabby booklet that outlines each day's training. A sample week goes like this:

Monday morning, 10 miles (the last two fast)

Monday afternoon, one hour

Tuesday morning, 6 miles

Tuesday afternoon, one hour

Wednesday morning, 12 to 15 miles

Wednesday afternoon, one hour

Thursday morning, 9 miles

Thursday afternoon, one hour

Friday morning, 3 miles

Friday afternoon, one hour slow

Saturday morning, 10 miles

Saturday afternoon, free

Sunday morning, 18 miles

Sunday afternoon, free.

That's about 111 miles in seven days.

His race strategy is this: "If I'm running twelve miles, the first six miles I run slow. The next six miles depends on the other runners. If all the runners are strong, I follow until they get weak."

*****

Through all of this—the races, the sprints, the long runs—a man named Pay Sok gives Bonthoeun petty cash when he needs it. He's a half manager, half coach who times Bonthoeun's sprints and offers moral support. Sok has never studied the science of running and training, although he ran half marathons when he was younger. "In high school I always raced with my friends, then I became a runner." Now he coaches eight athletes, including Bonthoeun—the only athlete the government pays him to coach—for sixty dollars a month. It isn't enough, so Sok has a second job as a soldier. "If I depend on only one job, I cannot live. It's not enough for my family. I also depend on my wife—she is a businesswoman."

Sok enjoys his role in the runner's life. "I always give money to Bonthoeun to feed his family or to buy petrol. I pity him very much, that's why I always help," he says. "I think Mok Bonthoeun works so hard because his family is so poor. They depend on him. He tries to train very hard. He is the best in Cambodia." He thinks Bonthoeun has the stamina, strength, and skill required of a prized runner. "In the future he can become the best."

*****

Back at the old stadium, it's almost 8 a.m., and the sun beats on Bonthoeun's sweat-soaked back. He finishes the first sprint in 1:07. Girls still hang on the sidelines, watching him run.

"Ooh, it's fast! I planned 1:15. Very tired. Rest one minute, go."

He scratches the cinders with a plastic spoon, marking his laps. By the fourth lap, he's tuckered. By lap 7, Sok arrives on his moto, long after Bonthoeun has given up hope for a breakfast. The coach is dressed in smart green dress slacks, brown shirt, leather sandals, gold watch on his wrist, silver pen in his pocket. He carries a cell phone and a brief case. He stops at the finish line, pulls out a stopwatch, and notes the time.

On lap 9, Bonthoeun is too tired to speak, and on 10, he's ready to quit. He unties his spikes, peels off his ragged socks, and treads softly, barefoot, along the track's grassy edge to cool down. Meanwhile, Sok times other sprinters around the track.

When Bonthoeun finishes, he stands atop the trackside bleachers and wraps a checkered krama around his waist. He slides off his shorts and changes into dress pants. He shoves both pairs of shoes in his bag and dresses in a clean white-collared shirt over his salty back. Then he eases into flip-flops. He stretches. And he waits for Sok, for the breakfast he knows he will finally receive.

When Sok is ready, he leads Bonthoeun across the track to a soup stall. The runner orders a hearty bowl—rice noodles and egg noodles mixed with slices of raw beef that cook in the boiling soup. He dips his meat into a tiny dish of orange chile sauce. He makes juice from sugar, hot water, and a fresh wedge of lime. The shopkeeper grins.

"I eat breakfast here," Bonthoeun says, "but I don't pay her. I owe her. Because she thinks I am a poor man."

But this morning, like many, Pay Sok pays.

"He is a good man for me," Bonthoeun says. "When I become a famous runner, he will be famous too. I run for him, and he works for me."

Sok agrees with this assessment of their relationship. He fetches a cup of tea, then rushes off on his motorbike for a Buddhist celebration at his neighborhood temple.

Bonthoeun stays behind briefly, finishing his soup before heading home across the city, through honking traffic and clouds of smog, until his second run of the day in late afternoon. He'll be back on the track tomorrow morning; whether he will have breakfast, he doesn't know. But he won't stop running. It's what he does.

"I will run until I'm old, until I can't walk, until I cannot go. I think this is my right."

Next page: Mok Bonthoeun, one of Cambodia's best top-level runners, practices in rough conditions around the capital, Phnom Penh.

6. Running on Empty - 2003

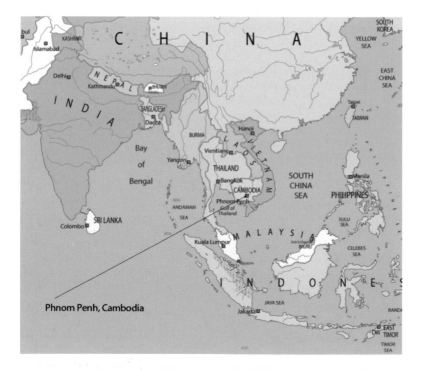

Phnom Penh, Cambodia

7. Om's Love – 1998, 1999

It's our first week in Cambodia, in 1998, and Jerry and I sit at a small Irish pub drinking weak beer and chatting with a few of my fellow editors. I just started work at an English-language newspaper, The Cambodia Daily. Perhaps I mention I want to learn Khmer; perhaps that's how Om enters our conversation. I don't recall exactly, but I do recall a friend named Jeff telling us about Professor Kang Om, a jovial man whose number is scrawled on the dry-erase board hanging in the living room of the house we all share. Professor Om will gladly teach us Khmer, Jeff says. Om is a fascinating man who has a plenitude of stories—as most Cambodians do. According to Om's resume, he spent 1975 to 1979—the Khmer Rouge years—working as a slave-farmer.

I have no inkling that evening that Professor Om will become a trusted friend, a confidante, a bottomless fount of information I will consult through the years. I have no idea then that his shy teenage son, Sok Chea, will go on to study sociology in college and become my faithful translator. I can't picture Sok Chea whisking me around the city on a borrowed motorbike, helping me through interviews with doctors, monks, mahouts, and a princess. It will all be possible through Professor Om. A relationship with him, I learn, transcends time and spans generations. That's his nature.

*****

We call that number on the dry-erase board, and Om quickly becomes our mentor. He comes to our house every week, to teach us words. Jerry and I sit with him at a round table beneath a giant carving of elephants, chariots, and godkings, done in the ancient Angkor style. We gaze through French doors, over purple bougainvillea, watching palm trees shift in the breeze and squatter kids playing in dirt across the street. Om teaches us names for all the things around us.

He believes in teaching casual conversation more than formal language structure. He tells us the important words, the words two American journalists will need for hailing moto-taxis, buying garlic in the market, or alerting the neighborhood to a thief on the prowl, which later comes in handy.

*****

Professor Om comes the day before our six-month wedding anniversary, our buon ting ay riep ca.

"Ting ay saik, buon ting ay riep ca yeung," I say. "Tomorrow is our anniversary." Just six months, but Jerry and I will celebrate nonetheless.

"Ah? Really?" Om asks, in that way of his, with sparkling eyes and a jiggling belly. "I remember when I was married just six months," Om says, slipping into a clarion of recollection. In fact, he remembers very, very clearly.

He was married March 23, 1977, during the years when Pol Pot and the Khmer Rouge herded cityfolk to the countryside in their efforts to create an agrarian state. They forced everyone to work like slaves. The educated fled or denied their identities, because those who didn't were killed. In less than four years, some 1.7 million people died of starvation, disease, or a hoe smacked against the head. Children betrayed parents, neighbors killed friends—most had to or they, too, would be killed. Some relished the killing, and prospered.

Even now, the memories of that time still torment the country, and the psychological consequences of genocide have been passed to new generations. Listen to the stories, and it's easy to see why. A woman at my paper clawed her way to safety through fields of bones when she was just seven years old. Another woman, across the street, has a divot in her head, the track of a murderous hoe swung a little too softly. She also says she saw soldiers rip the liver from her father's gut and eat it raw. Psychologists say many Cambodians have never properly dealt with the traumas they endured.

Yet somehow in that deep crevasse of horror, Professor Om found a miraculous love. He didn't just survive the Khmer Rouge; he came away a cherished man, with a wife who loves him as he loves her.

Thirty-three couples were united on March 23, 1977, a day the Khmer Rouge chose for weddings they had arranged. "Everyone was scared," Om recalls. True love, sro-lanh, is hard to come by under such arrangements. But there was no choice. The people were told they would marry partners selected for them: no options. Om sat among the other slave-farmers as the Khmer Rouge leaders called names one by one and assigned each person a partner. People feared a match with someone legless or armless or blind, for such a spouse couldn't work in the fields and most certainly would die. No one wanted to marry a stranger when he or she loved another, but rebellion meant risking one's life.

So Om and the others sat in fear, awaiting their call. The Khmer Rouge leaders segregated the group into "17s" and "18s." The 17s were those who had been forced from Phnom Penh to the countryside in the mass exodus of April 17, 1975, that fateful day when the Khmer Rouge stormed the city and laid the roots of genocide. A ghost town emerged where the capital once thrived, and so it remained through the regime. The 17s were intellectuals, professionals, monks, and officials; they didn't support the Khmer Rouge but were forced to submit. The 18s had joined ranks much earlier, after March 18, 1970, when Cambodia's King Norodom Sihanouk was stripped of his power. They already were living the Khmer Rouge life in rural villages. From 1975 to 1979, the 17s worked the fields and frequently died of starvation; the 18s were favored and generally fared better.

Om was a 17.

In his telling, he recalls those uncertain moments when he raised his hand to learn of the woman he would have to love, his praw poon thmei, his new wife. But Om's karma fared well that day, and they called the name of a distant relative named Top Kiel. She, too, was a 17. They knew and liked each other well, though they couldn't divulge such a secret. Om and Top Kiel suited each other nicely. For them, there would be no spouse-swapping in the night, no rendez-vous with a true love. Some couples had clandestine affairs behind the back of the organization, the awnka. Those caught were bludgeoned to death, their bodies left to rot in sweltering fields. The awnka rarely wasted money on bullets or time on burial. Leaving corpses in the open also left a clear message for the living.

Om says the thirty-three couples that day shared one wedding feast, with brides facing grooms at the table. When the eating was done, each couple was granted a three-day honeymoon, a tiny reprieve. Newlyweds retreated to the wife's family home, generally a one-room bamboo shack housing a bushel of kin. "Heh, heh, heh," Om chuckles, recounting the story of one family whose three daughters returned with three husbands—and three marriages to consummate in one cramped shanty.

When the honeymoon ended, Om and his wife resumed a divided life. Working men and women lived in separate communes, forced away from each other and away from their families. A ten-kilometer footpath linked their lives. On the tenth, twentieth, and thirtieth days of each month, the Khmer Rouge permitted Om to travel that distance, a malnourished and delirious trudge under oppressive skies, to meet his bride. They shared a few amorous hours before he set out again to greet the 6 a.m. start of his workday, ten kilometers back—so far from his darling, his owen. "I was very thin," he laughs, clutching his round belly, remembering those years of near starvation.

Professor Om says he "never had, never had" an anniversary like ours. He says he takes Top Kiel to dinner on the twenty-third day of every March, but she prefers not to remember. She likes to think instead of the present. Both Kang Om and Top Kiel, in their own ways, recognize their serendipity, their luck. Theirs is a chance sro-lanh that defied the odds.

Professor Kang Om with his wife, Top Kiel,
saddle up on their motorbike in Phnom Penh.

More than twenty years after their wedding, Professor Om says, he still calls Top Kiel his *owen*—a rarity, he explains. Cambodians typically identify a spouse through the name of the firstborn child. "M'day Sok Chea" she should be. The mother of Sok Chea, their eldest son, a grown man himself now.

But instead, Top Kiel remains Kang Om's *owen*, his sweetheart, in a union that flourished amid evil.

Phnom Penh, Cambodia

8. Baking Bread, Making a Living - 2010

It was 1998 when Jerry first visited the 7 January Bread Co., named for the day the Vietnamese army rolled into Phnom Penh and ousted the Khmer Rouge. The factory is tucked inside a big building, blackened with the soot of continuous fires. Young men hustled through the blazing heat of the giant ovens that cooked the capital's popular sandwich bread and breakfast baguettes. I wasn't along on that story, at that time, but I remember Jerry telling me about the light. And I remember a particular photo showing a shaft of sunlight beaming down to a tray of bread. That image stuck in my mind for years, pulling me back to Cambodia long after we had moved on.

Move ahead a dozen years. It's a muggy morning at the sort of hour when slanted orange sunlight burns on the brink of hot months to come. We ride up to the factory entrance and peek inside. It's still here. Most everything looks the same, Jerry says, as though no time passed in a span of twelve years. The young men, of course, are different, but the conditions haven't changed—except the light, if anything, has diminished. And the ovens have nearly doubled in size.

We chat a bit with twelve-year-old Mouy Sang, the owner's daughter, who says the factory uses a simple recipe of flour, salt, yeast, eggs, and water, just as her grandfather did when he started the business in 1984.

"When my father retired, I started to be the boss," says her father, Tang Pao Sreng. Business has grown through the years, though "the profit is not good." His baguettes sell for 400 riel (10 cents) apiece, but sidewalk vendors up the price to $1 or more per sandwich. His bread goes all over town, and he bakes as many loaves as needed. "If someone orders a lot, we make more than ten thousand pieces of bread a day," he says. "If someone orders five thousand pieces, we make five thousand pieces."

The factory is divided in half—one room dark and oppressive, with four giant ovens, each nearly the size of a single-car garage; the other room lighter and airier, with a two-story ceiling and a stainless steel Macadams Baking Systems industrial oven. Ancient cobwebs are dipped in dust and dripping from the rafters. Three fire extinguishers hang on the wall, almost unrecognizable beneath a blanket of soot. Their utility at this point is debatable.

This place smells human, of yeast and sweat and young men at work. It's the scent of necessity. Most of the twenty to thirty employees come from other provinces where the only job is farming for sustenance, which falls short of need. Here, they live on-site and earn two dollars a day, seven days a week. The bulk of their money goes back home.

A thin older man sits beside the doorway, weighing packages of yeast and salt. Around the corner, young workers stack long, rectangular trays of uncooked loaves while a colleague sprays a fine film of water across the dough.

In the corner, by the door, sunlight streams through a storm of flour as two boys twirl a giant tub beneath a rotating mixer. Little dollops of dough fly from the tub, splattering the room. An orange cat, snoozing beside a pink Buddhist shrine, lifts its head in a look of utter contentment. Jerry asks Tang Pao Sreng about the feline's proficiency in catching mice. He laughs. "Oooh, no! That's a lazy cat."

A couple of boxes hold the morning's mistakes. "These are burnt so we keep for pig or chicken feed," Tang Pao Sreng says. He delivers the crusty loaves to his relatives around Phnom Penh.

Each tray of bread requires thirty minutes in the oven. Every few minutes, workers in mitts twirl the trays in graceful maneuvers that assure uniform baking. Meanwhile, two clean, woven mats are spread across the floor near the doorway, and a basket the size of a bathtub is placed on its side. When the bread is done, the trays are dumped, and hundreds of loaves cascade across the mats. The bread crackles in fresh heat, popping like Rice Krispies in milk. Five trays, six trays, seven, eight, nine are emptied beside the little shrine, as though each loaf is presented as a gift to the gods.

Workers squat on the edge of the mat, arranging bread into symmetrical piles, then filling the giant basket for delivery across town. I chat with Hong Heng, twenty-three, as he counts and moves the loaves. He arrived five years ago from Prey Veng province. "I came here to make a living. I was jobless there." Every month, he sends money back to his parents. He works two shifts a day—3 a.m. to 7 a.m. and 9 a.m. to 5 p.m. The job is OK, he says, but he tires of the single thing he makes. "I work with bread every day. I don't want to eat it."

Jerry and I stay a few hours that morning, then return two days later, as employees unload a truck full of flour. Each man carries two sacks in the crook of his neck. Sweat follows a path down one man's tattooed arm. Meanwhile, another worker heaves an axe, breaking one log at a time into useful segments of wood to feed the belching fires.

I talk with a young man named Kum Orn, who comes from the nearby province of Takeo. He used to make palm juice, not a lucrative living. So he moved to Phnom Penh "to have the city life," meaning a steady job. He tells me his story while spinning dough in the dark corner of this photogenic room. I look around and think this place has charisma, with shafts of light that scream through tiny holes in the roof. Smoke billows through narrow openings between two walls. It's hard to imagine a setting with more picturesque light.

But I realize my perception of beauty is that of an observer, not a worker. I don't shape wads of dough into little loaves, day after day, in a monotonous cycle. It's hot, it's stifling, it's repetitious. I wonder what Kum Orn thinks of the light in this room.

"If we had more light, it would be too hot," he says.

But is it pretty?

"I don't know, I never think about that."

I wonder what he thinks of my questions, or the fact that I'm here, looking around. I wonder what he sees in this place, which I find intriguing. Does Kum Orn think this factory is interesting?

"Yes, he says. "It's interesting to me—because I have a job here."

8. Baking Bread, Making a Living - 2010

Left and below: Workers load a rack of fresh dough loaves into a wood-fired oven at the 7 January Bread Company. The factory, tucked in an alley behind the Royal Palace, is named after the day the Vietnamese invaded Cambodia, driving the Khmer Rouge from power. For 27 years, the factory has churned out thousands of loaves of French-style bread daily. French colonialists brought bread to Cambodia, but the Cambodians have incorporated it into their diet on their own terms. While rice remains Cambodia's staple food, bread is common fare in cities and towns.

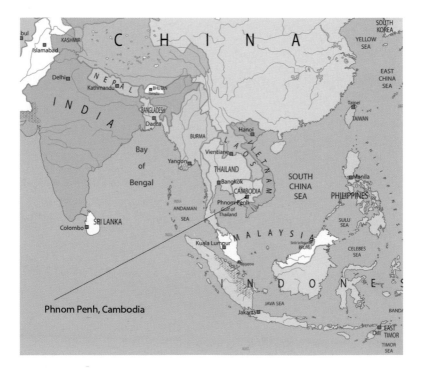

Phnom Penh, Cambodia

9. The Dancer King - 2004

It's the tail end of October 2004, and much of the world is tuned to the election drama of George Bush and John Kerry. But politics elsewhere take no intermission, and Cambodia enthrones a dancer. Norodom Sihamoni is named the country's first new king in half a century, thus beginning a fresh chapter in the country's saga of trouble.

A coronation is on tap, and we're invited. Or, more accurately: we're allowed to attend.

The 51-year-old bald-headed, ballet-dancing bachelor, the son of former king Norodom Sihanouk, returns home to Phnom Penh after years in Paris, where he held a permanent slot as ambassador to UNESCO.

Though friends and relatives say this man lived a modest lifestyle in the French capital, his office in the Sixteenth Arrondissement lies an eternity from the squalor that engulfs his homeland. He may have chosen to ride the Metro to work like ordinary Parisians, but his new posting returns him to a palace set among millions of the world's poorest people. It's the same palace where the Khmer Rouge imprisoned him and his family, killing five of his siblings during their brutal regime. That was the horror from which he fled, eventually alighting in Paris.

Sihamoni's father, Sihanouk, abdicates the throne on the eve of his eighty-second birthday, citing ill health. A Throne Council is hastily assembled and Sihamoni is quickly chosen as successor. Many describe the whole affair as a

Sihanouk dance to secure an heir while he still can. Rumor says that Prime Minister Hun Sen would like nothing better than to end the monarchy, a group with whom he has never gotten along.

Sihamoni, the faithful son, comes home as requested, accepting his new role with trembling hands but perfect poise. He vows to "never live apart from the beloved people."

But the new king inherits a country in shambles. Cambodia's millions are among Asia's poorest, averaging less than a dollar a day in income. They have the region's highest HIV-infection rate, and almost none of the basics of a democratic society—law and order, education, infrastructure. Street mobs punish alleged criminals when the cops and courts do not. Corruption is notorious and bribes are expected. Government slots are bought in cash and traded for power. Millions of dollars in international aid have disappeared through the years. And the United Nations calls the country a potential terrorism breeding ground. Beyond all that, the Khmer Rouge left a nation scarred, both physically and mentally. Cambodia has about twenty psychiatrists, but millions in need.

Indeed, presiding over the Kingdom of Cambodia may very well prove to be Sihamoni's toughest dance. Perhaps that's why the new monarch's hands shake ever so slightly and the vein above his right temple bulges visibly as he makes his vows. "As from this happy and solemn day I shall devote my body and soul to the service of the people and the nation, pursuing the exceptional work accomplished by my august father."

That man was one of the twentieth century's longest-lasting political players, outliving most all his friends and foes—among them, Charles de Gaulle, Kim Il Sung, JFK, LBJ, Nixon, Lon Nol, Pol Pot, Chairman Mao, Ho Chi Minh, and Deng Xiaoping. Though the Cambodian Constitution stipulates the king "shall reign but shall not govern," few would deny the monarchy's hand in political affairs.

The French enthroned Sihanouk in 1941, thinking him a malleable player. No such luck. The young king wrested independence from France, then abdicated for a life of politics. He somersaulted through years of turmoil and political alliances. Sihanouk named, outlawed, and eventually sided with the Khmer Rouge, when the Vietnam War spilled into Cambodia. That alliance ended after the Khmer Rouge took control, imprisoned the royal family, killed several of

Sihanouk's children, and instigated a genocide that left an estimated 1.7 million Cambodians dead.

When the Vietnamese ousted the Khmer Rouge from power in 1979, Sihanouk created a government in exile and again allied with the Khmer Rouge to fight against the Vietnamese-backed government and its star, current Prime Minister Hun Sen. Peace accords were signed in 1991, though the Khmer Rouge civil war continued. Enter the UN, a flawed election, Sihanouk's rethroning in 1993, the eventual collapse of the Khmer Rouge from within, and a decade of brilliantly corrupt politics.

Cambodians often call Sihanouk their beloved ruler, a father whose beatific portrait still adorns homes and offices. Yet others are not so enamored of the man. The most outspoken will say they blame the former king for Cambodia's long-term troubles. In the past decade, Sihanouk has spent more time in Beijing and Pyongyang than in Phnom Penh's Royal Palace: people know he's gone because the palace lights are snuffed when the king is away. He has departed for medical care, political protest, and "self-imposed exile," frequently criticizing his country's government, still run by Hun Sen. To some, the king's absence is abandonment. They would rather he stayed and fought the bully government for his people. Instead, he left the people to wrestle their demons alone.

This is a country that accords its king divine status. While Cambodians hate to insult their heritage, the most vocal ask: Would a godking allow such excruciating poverty and institutional corruption? Would he permit the continued rule of a prime minister largely viewed as an ogre, one who cares more for his Vietnamese friends than for his own people? Would not a godking intervene?

These are the questions Cambodians quietly ask about their new King Sihamoni. In reality, they know little about this man who has spent so much time abroad—attending high school in Prague, studying cinematography in North Korea, and practicing choreography in Paris. Some think Sihamoni more foreign than Khmer. Local chatter wonders why the new monarch has neither wife at his side nor hair on his head (this fashion of Paris is a sign of mourning among Buddhists). Some hope he's a good Buddhist, "married to the people." His vows to stick to home are a grand and welcome divergence from his father's style. But most Cambodians, a patient lot, will wait and see whether Sihamoni is up to the task of dancing through the Cambodian mud. It's hard to dance in the mud.

*****

"It has only been a few days. It is too early," says a Phnom Penh moto-taxi driver named Thierry. Cambodia's current government resembles Communism, he says, "but I am a democrat." He wants to know whether the new king will uphold his political ideals.

"If he is good, he must fix his country's problems," says a restaurateur on the Phnom Penh riverfront, who believes the true kings were Suryavarman, Jayavarman, and their fellow architects of the Angkor empire a thousand years ago. Everyone else has let him down. The restaurateur thinks Sihanouk should have stopped the political impasse that left Cambodia without a functional government for nearly a year after the July 2003 election. In the end, a coalition was formed between Hun Sen's party and the opposition. Hun Sen secured five more years at the helm, and the people's outlook reached another low. "Cambodian democracy is not real," the restaurateur tells me, explaining that loudmouthed Cambodians who oppose the status quo ultimately face three options: exile, arrest, or death. "I do not like to speak against my king," he says, but he wonders whether Sihamoni can—or will—stand against such systematic wrongs.

*****

Yet none of that skepticism is apparent when Sihamoni visits Kompong Speu province, the first of his promised meetings in the countryside, just four days after his coronation. There, he navigates a dusty courtyard, greeting thousands of Cambodians who left home and school and farm to see him. It takes the king more than half an hour to reach his podium, so many hands does he shake and babies does he cuddle. He wears a simple gray suit, bowing and smiling, blessing the aged and disabled.

It's a journey up the aisle, followed by a short speech, strikingly similar to hundreds Sihanouk made before him. Sihamoni acts as expected—which is precisely why many Cambodians wonder whether he will, in years to come, flit across the royal stage and into the wings of another country, a mere shadow of his father.

*****

In those last days of October, Phnom Penh prepares for an event that hasn't happened in fifty years. Red carpets are unfurled, the palace is painted, and a royal crown and sword are ordered, to replace those lost during Pol Pot's time. The Cambodian flag flutters through a typically tropical breeze. And Sihamoni's portrait is raised—in some cases, alone; in others, right beside his aged father's.

The three-day gala begins with official and religious rites—lots of candles and incense and prayers by the country's top monks. Sihamoni's parents bathe him with holy water from the mountains near Angkor, in a ceremony invoking the divine spirits of ancient kings for their latest incarnation. He ascends the throne to the sounds of traditional Khmer music and the blowing of conch shells, following a parade of Brahmin priests carrying all manner of traditional, ceremonial offerings—a horsetail whip, a house cat, fresh vegetables, and Buddha statues. After accepting his duties before an audience of dignitaries, monks, and journalists, Sihamoni signs the pardons of eighty-eight prisoners. Then he carefully removes his spectacles and bows to a bevy of cameramen, mouthing: "Merci beaucoup. Thank you."

That night, as on every night of the coronation ceremonies, masses of people swarm the Phnom Penh riverfront, picnicking and gathering to see the palace aglow. Fireworks crackle in the night sky, causing several Cambodians to jump from the memory of ear-cracking booms that, in recent times, meant disturbance and death.

On the last day of coronation festivities, Sihamoni appears solemn while praying in the palace's Silver Pagoda, so named for its floor of five thousand silver tiles. It's a small, austere ceremony. The King wears loafers and his guards dress in silk suits with fraying gold threads. A couple of bodyguards tsk-tsk a neglected flowerbed, and the scent of a leaky sewer hose tinges the air. But the new monarch smiles a lot and leaves the impression of a very nice and gentle man.

After prayers, the king pays homage to his ancestors' stupas on the palace grounds, carefully laying jasmine wreaths on each tastefully carved memorial. Then he kneels and prays some more, clasping a matchbox, lighting candles to the monarchs who came before him and stuffing incense sticks into silver chalices. Palm trees rustle in the background and swarms of pigeons flap overhead.

Sihamoni exits the palace gate to a waiting convertible and thousands of soldiers, police officers, and schoolchildren who dutifully wave flags and posters in his honor. After a short public ride in the Mercedes, he gives his first speech to the nation while standing beneath a golden parasol.

When he finishes, the throngs quickly clear and dozens of scavengers comb the littered square between the Royal Palace and Tonle Sap River. One boy stuffs a squashed loaf of bread into his mouth. Others collect the sticks tacked to the backs of Sihamoni posters; they will use the wood for cooking-fires.

A ten-year-old boy named Peak Kaday collects recyclable plastic water bottles, filling a rice sack as tall as his body. He could earn 1,000 riel, about 25 cents, for that sack. But it costs that same amount for a motorbike-taxi home, so he begs for more money. When I ask what he thinks of his new king, Peak Kaday gazes across the lawn to a giant portrait of Sihamoni's bald head, hanging from the palace. "He's French," the boy says, before hoisting his bag and trundling on.

That night, the square fills again with Phnom Penh residents who were not allowed to attend the king's speech and accompanying ceremonies, but find his coronation an excuse to party anyway. In front of the palace, where each corner and every angle is lit with a hundred lightbulbs, women and kids clutch baskets atop their heads and bushels in their laps, filled with snacks for sale—banana fritters, fried spiders, steamed taro, roasted peanuts, handmade spring rolls, pickled mango. A swarm of humanity jams the riverfront for hours. For the next two nights, just north of the Royal Palace, music warbles through loudspeakers and floodlights illuminate a small stage in the park. And there, Cambodians dance a ballet for the love of their king.

But on the third night, everything changes. For quite some time, the street lights fail to turn on. The park is dark. And the palace returns to its familiar murk.

Right and following page: View from the coronation ceremony for Cambodian King Sihamoni in 2004.

9. The Dancer King - 2004

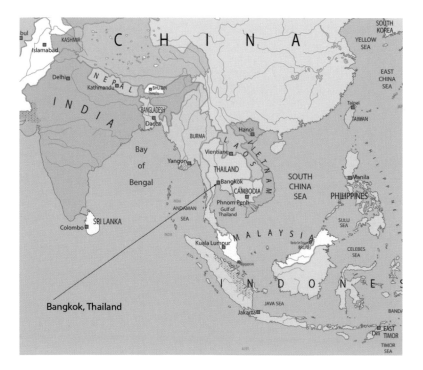

Bangkok, Thailand

10. The Splendors and Smells of Bangkok - 2004

Ah, Bangkok. I can smell it now, the thick stew of diesel secretions, the stench of sweltering bodies, a potpourri of fried meats in hot woks, a swirl of rotting fruit and swamp air. The cloud hits as soon as I pass through the glass airport doors. Eau d'Bangkok, stout and sticky.

We've landed in that city scores of times—first at Don Muang; now at Suvarn-abhumi, the giant new jetport built over an old swamp. Add to that all the bus rides in, bus rides out, train rides in, train rides out, and nights curled on hard airport seats sized for Asian tushes. Bangkok is something of a third or fourth home to us. We know it better than most American cities, better than the Milwaukee of my roots. Bangkok is our hub. Not where we live—but where we get things done.

There are reasons to love Bangkok, reasons to hate it, and most people profess rigid opinions one way or the other. I find little in life to be black and white, particularly not a city of such colossal dimensions. I hate that it's a haven of human trafficking, a place where kids are trucked across the border from Burma, Laos, Cambodia: forced to sell flowers, candy, or themselves on the street, lest their boss beat them (so survivors tell me). I hate the go-go bars of Patpong with their pudgy-faced clients sweating over sweet young prostitutes, male and female, whom they buy for cheap. I hate the choking air.

But marvels and awe: I love the Jade Buddha, jeweled stupas, royal barges, and homes of teak (though fewer and fewer of those every year); the somnolence of people at prayer. World cuisines sold for half their worldly worth. Street food on a stick for pennies. The green curry Jerry adores, the jungle soup I prefer, the som tam we both inhale until our stomachs revolt. I rarely have to ask for it spicier; it comes that way naturally.

If it's shopping you like—silk, silver, CDs, cheap wigs, Chinese tchotchkes, nunchakus, bongs, Rolex, Armani—if you can imagine it, someone is selling the real thing or a knockoff in highbrow malls or sidewalk markets.

What I love most is the serendipity, the entropy. Deep in a maze of klongs and Indian cloth stalls, there's a little Nepali place where a dish of dhal costs about fifty cents. Go there and hunch over an elfin table in a room redolent of curry. I love that place, and I love the way one finds it; in a Bangkok stupor, wandering here and there, up and over little bridges in the gaps between clustered shops, the people, the colors, the sounds and vibrations, bearded men smoking, scarfed women serving tea, deeper into that maze until—there it is. A little spot of wonder. But then, to find it again: that's the mystery that fashions my Bangkok.

But we are no longer tourists here. We stopped visiting the galleries, the temples, the halls of royal regalia a few dozen boarding passes ago. Bangkok is no longer Krung Thep to us, the "City of Angels." It's the home of photo shops, office-supply stores, computer malls, FedEx carriers, and Jerry's photo agency, OnAsia, bless their business hearts.

We see Bangkok through the sweaty pits and harried eyes of rat-racers. We see it while huffing up Phra Athit Road (The Road of the Sun that runs east-west) to catch the No. 15 bus to a film shop off Silom Road. It's a smelly, belching hog that rarely comes. The 82 rolls around the corner every five minutes, but the 15? Only Buddha knows where it goes.

If it's not the 15, it's the air-conditioned 511, a double-hauler with a center built like an accordion that ripples over pavement. This one heads to Sukhumvit, toward OnAsia; or toward Panthip, the computer mall. Somehow, I'm always sopping when we board the 511—caught in the sun and sweaty; or caught in a downpour, clothes clinging to my legs in the freezing bowels of the bus.

If it's not a bus, it's the Chao Phraya ferry, with the guy in back whistling to the driver up front: Tweet! Back up! Tweettweet! Now forward! TaWEET! You hit the pier! Screeching whistle, spluttering smoke, bilge water. It's a scenic cruise through the city's heart—for those who don't have to do it every day. Earplugs help.

From the ferry, it's up the steps to the Sky Train (BTS stop: Thaksin), which takes us to the photo lab (BTS stop: Chong Nonsi, northeast exit), the digital printing shop (BTS stop: Chong Nonsi, southwest exit), the film shop (BTS stop: Ratchathewi), or OnAsia (BTS stop: first Silom, then moved to Chitlom, now moved to Surasak) on an alternate route. BTS is a breeze. It's the most comfortable trek through Bangkok, a smooth and quiet zip among skyscrapers.

But life outside is different. One day, Jerry needs a print from the digital lab. I accompany him (BTS stop, Chong Nonsi). We arrive at the shop and discover his CD is damaged. Back to OnAsia he goes (old office, four BTS stops away: Chit Lom). I stay behind, get myself an ice cream, and watch the world below. There, the platform overlooks a squatter camp, dozens of filthy shanties amid heaps of scrap metal. I watch a young man scrambling through weeds, picking handfuls for dinner. He tugs at a tree over the fence and comes away with a branch of edible leaves. Laundry hangs among boards and broken toilets. A resident vendor sells fruit from a cart outside the fence. But all around me on that BTS platform: black pants, pressed shirts, high heels, designer suits, cell phones, and the look of money.

When Jerry returns, we walk to the lab and pass a one-eyed beggar with skin scarred by fire, dressed in rumpled clothes that look as though he hasn't changed in weeks. We put a few baht into his cup and ask where he is from. "Korat," he says, smiling, naming a town in eastern Thailand. He speaks English and asks about us. He shakes our hands vigorously and thanks us for stopping to chat.

And then, we are back on the move.

Transfer is always a bustle, a sprint from one train to the next, a jog to the dock. But once aboard, it's a sleepy slide to stasis. Minutes amble by, then hours; passengers sit and stare. Some snore, some drool; at some point, nearly everyone ogles a phone, sending messages to friends across town or just across the bus—texting is a premier Asian pastime. Few people actually read; it is not Thai culture. Waiting is. "It is a dreadful sort of idleness, an unbearable tedium, to sit motionless like this, in a state of mental numbness, not really doing anything," Polish journalist Ryszard Kapuscinski once wrote. He knew it well, had seen it the world over. Thailand embodies that inertia of waiting. "Everywhere, that same sight—people sitting motionless for hours on end, on old chairs, on bits of plank, on plastic crates, in the shade of poplars and mango trees, leaning against the walls of slums, against fences and frames…" Jerry calls it the hammock culture.

Occasionally, I demand an escape from the tedium. I put my foot down (firmly, in dog doo), and I tell Jerry we must do something fun. Something sophisticated and citylike.

One Saturday evening we dress up and board the boat, heading not for an office or shop, but the State Tower (River ferry stop: Oriental Pier), a high-rise that for years was a Bangkok ogre. It was one of many semi- or fully abandoned buildings left undone after the 1997 Asian economic crash, massive gaping holes in the skyline, monuments to failure. But things change, particularly here on the corner of Silom and Charoen Krung.

*****

Take the elevator to the sixty-fourth floor, all the way up, turn left and left again. You're now atop a wide, stately staircase overlooking a restaurant completely open to the sky. Stand still and catch your breath—not that you have a choice. The scene is breathtaking. Then carefully navigate the steps and strut to the bar on the far side. Order a cocktail and stretch your midriff over the glass wall separating you and pavement, sixty-four floors below. Note the tiny net eight feet down that might catch your cell phone: you'd fly right through. Order another drink (because you'll decide to use credit tonight, this is an occasion). Nibble a few cashews and take the waitress up on an offer of free martini samples (something else I love, so many free samples in Thailand). Watch all of the cars jammed on the expressways far below.

Then advance to a Mediterranean dinner. It's a beautiful name, for a beautiful restaurant—Sirocco. But there is irony in its name: an elegant Bangkok affair named after a hot, oppressive wind.

You sit in that wind and savor plates of buffalo mozzarella, avocado, couscous, olives. Seared tuna in black pepper. Grilled ostrich with sun-dried chile chutney. Your brain momentarily dredges up the Murray Head chestnut: "One night in Bangkok and the world's your oyster…"

Finish the meal with ruby port and another view from the bar. Just look at all those people below. Six million? Ten million? No one really knows, actually.

When the evening closes, descend to Earth and pass through the State Tower lobby. Exit to the street, where the turgid reek of Bangkok slams your nose. Look at all those taxis, buses, tuk-tuks. All those people cradled in dark alleys and all those scraggly dogs sniffing through piles of garbage. You're back on common Bangkok ground.

You walk a few blocks, then take a water taxi back to your hotel (River ferry stop: Phra Athit) until the next morning, when the journey begins again.

View of Bangkok, Thailand, from a metropolitan city bus crossing town.

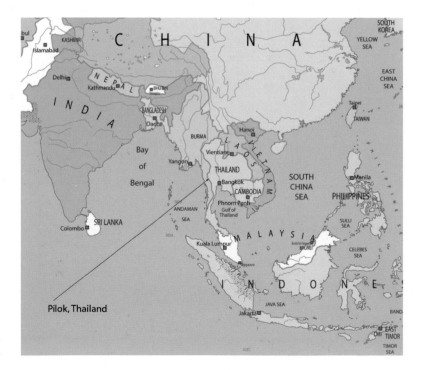

Pilok, Thailand

11. An Oven in the Jungle - 2005

It's one of the dumber things we do—heading down that dark road on foot. But circumstance offers few options.

We rent a jeep in Kanchanaburi and drive all afternoon toward the Burmese border. We watch the world grow slower, emptier, as we climb through mountains, past lonely villages, past farmers lugging their nightly firewood from the forest. It's dusk when we reach Pilok, the last little town before our destination. There is no one around.

We've come to see Aunty Glen, a sixty-seven-year-old Australian with a cherubic face who lives somewhere out there beneath the canopy of trees, one of Thailand's last remaining great patches of wildlands. Aunty Glen followed her Thai husband, Somsak, to a tin mine in the middle of nowhere forty years ago. The industry collapsed twenty years later, and her beloved died in 1994. But Aunty Glen stayed on.

Or so we've been told. We've never met Aunty Glen, but a friend in Bangkok tells us we must see this woman who runs a homestay in the jungle. She has an oven. She bakes cakes. They're the best in Thailand.

Aunty Glen has no phone. We've been calling her son all afternoon, but he's in Bangkok and still we can't get through. So here we are in Pilok, on the brink of night, on the brink of a monsoon storm. We look around the shuttered town, then aim the jeep at a narrow dirt track. It must be the way. We arrived on the only other road leaving town.

We drive and drive, up and around steep curves with slippery muck beneath the tires. Daylight dissipates to a wet black. The headlights capture little beyond the rocky road: one side is the dirt wall of a hill, slowly turning to mud in the rain and oozing onto the road. The other side drops off into an inky canyon.

And then we reach a point where we can go no farther—the road too steep, too muddy, too rocky, too slick. We have a frightening descent behind us to Pilok and unknown conditions ahead, two-wheel drive and bald tires. No rain for the moment, but the moon plays hide-and-seek with voluptuous clouds. We park in a clearing, grab our packs and flashlights, lock the doors behind us, and head downhill in our boots. Rocks and pebbles crunch beneath our feet. We tromp deep into the damp, black night.

It's only three kilometers, as far as we can discern, although it feels six times that distance before we meet a friendly Burmese family who guides us to a light in the dark. And there, with open arms, is Aunty Glen. She ushers us into her warm, dry kitchen of goodies.

The ranch house is a homey oasis of tchotchkes—wooden ducks, waving pandas, a puppy dog jigsaw puzzle, and a collection of crocheted pillowcases. Six Burmese youngsters gaze, google-eyed, at a Burmese TV show with Burmese subtitles as we pass through the living room.

It's late, we're exhausted, so Aunty Glen shows us to our room, the "VIP" quarters in a separate bungalow. It's a cozy abode with an eternal sort of dampness and the cleanest little bathroom the jungle ever did see. We sleep soundly that night with a wild creek gushing outside our windows.

*****

The next day, it rains steadily, so we explore beneath neon-colored umbrellas. Aunty Glen's property follows the creek. Several bamboo bungalows on raised platforms overlook the rushing water in a garden of ginger and hibiscus.

When we've soaked our feet and worked up a hunger, we return inside the great kitchen, flush with warm scents. Aunty Glen bakes a cake from scratch every day—chocolate, orange, carrot, banana, Bundt. We sit and nibble and chat. She's working on a book of her life stories—not because she's famous, she says, but because her stories are worth telling.

Glen met Somsak at home in Australia, where he had gone to study mining. Not long afterward, the two youngsters married, and the groom brought his new bride to Thailand. They arrived in Pilok in the 1960s, when the region bore little but jungle. They came in on some of the first vehicles to reach this stretch of Thailand's outback. There was no road; Somsak had to blast his own.

For years Pilok was a boomtown, home to six hundred or more workers. Many came from Burma. At first the Thai government didn't want Burmese laborers in the mine. But the company couldn't get Thais to do the hard work, she says, so the government relented.

The border lies just beyond Pilok, and just beyond Glen's home. She takes us there in her car, and the laid-back border guards let us step into Burma for a short walk down an empty, misty road. The authorities monitor seven posts along the border, Glen says, but "they have nothing to do."

Several years ago, when the Burmese cracked down on student uprisings, Glen says, two thousand protesters trudged through these jungles to safety. The UN got involved, sending most of the refugees to third-country hosts. But a few dozen exiles remained. They would not be here today, without Aunty Glen. She and Somsak even arranged to bring a Burmese monk to the valley. Before that, the people kept coming to her with problems she couldn't solve. The refugees loved the idea of inviting a monk, and they all helped to build him a modest temple nearby. "It was the fastest thing I ever saw them build," Glen says.

She is rooted here now. It's been more than a decade, but Glen still misses her husband deeply. Her eyes still dance when she says his name. Pilok was his life, her life—their life together. She couldn't leave this place.

Glen shares this valley with snakes, squirrels, bears, civets, and giant aged turtles. Two years before, she says, she spotted two tiger cubs playing by the roadside twenty kilometers from Pilok. In the third valley over lives an elephant herd, but they never come to Glen's home. One day, she asked a conservation officer at the nearby Thong Pha Phum National Park why she never sees those elephants in her valley. He told her the animals follow the same trails they and their predecessors have for generations. Year after year, they trace a segment of jungle they have always instinctively known.

The kitchen table is where Aunty Glen shares her stories. We gather there to listen and partake of a feast our hostess has cooked—whole fried fish, chicken curry, tofu with pork and onions, fried kale, chopped cucumbers with shallots and vinegar, ginger tea and—of course—an array of cakes. It's the way she's lived for decades now, here in Thailand's last valley before Burma.

The night looms black, the jungle thick with eerie sounds. But here inside this little house, we find Aunty Glen's welcome lights and the incongruous comfort of an oven in the jungle.

Aunty Glen runs a homestay near Pilok, Thailand, which is famous (in a local way) for her daily cakes. She employs many Burmese immigrants who ran across the nearby border following the 1988 Democracy uprising and subsequent crackdown in their country.

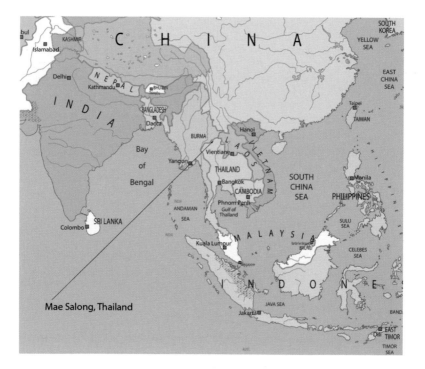

Mae Salong, Thailand

12. A Little Sip of Yunnan in Northern Thailand – 2008, 2010

We wake to a butter-colored sun cast across a valley of tea—neat, parallel rows that ribbon their way through rippled terrain. The air is sweet with frangipani. The sky spreads wide and clear with only a single cotton-candy cloud. I drink up the moment, alone on this balcony, indulging in this striking view. But then my head begins to swirl, and my mood turns slightly mean. Dammit! It's early and I need caffeine.

Ask, and I shall receive.

A young man shuffles across the tiles, quietly serving a pot of oolong, so crisp and clean with light floral hints, it's like drinking the morning light. My head clears, and I start to feel alive. More than alive. This tea is exceptionally good. It's said this local brew, here in the northern hills of Thailand, is better than its ancestral mother in Taiwan. Doi Mae Salong is a mountain made for tea—and for soldiers with a colorful past, tinged with their own addictions.

In the 1950s, anti-communist Kuomintang forces settled in these serpentine hills of the Golden Triangle. They'd been driven out of their homeland in Yunnan by Mao Zedong's communist army. They spread first into Burma's jungles, gaining reputations as fierce fighters and the region's heavyweight traders in opium (which helped fund their fight). When their presence in Burma became untenable (they were far better fighters than—and completely unafraid of—the Burmese Army), many Chiang Kai-shek loyalists were shepherded to Taiwan, headquarters of the KMT. But a band of soldiers known as the "Lost Army" remained in the region, settling across the border in Thailand. There, eventually, His Majesty the King granted refuge to the soldiers and their families in exchange for defense against the kingdom's own communist insurgents. Those battles lasted through the early 1980s.

But when they ended, the Thai government strongly encouraged the soldiers to kick the opium trade and grow alternative crops. Tea proved a logical contender; the high-value substitute crop provided a viable income as well as a direct link to their compatriots in Taiwan.

Today, Mae Salong remains a little enclave of Yunnan: red lanterns dangle from doorways, restaurants specialize in Yunnan ham, and the children here learn three languages in school—Thai, English, and Chinese. "I am Yunnanese. China," a vendor in the local morning market announces proudly, tapping her chest, before serving a spicy bowl of noodle stew with cabbage, pork, and chile. She offers two little cups of strong amber-colored tea, for free.

Tea is the reason most visitors come to Mae Salong. It's the spark of life for most residents, too. On weekends, locals gather around thick-slab wooden counters at tea shops scattered across town. People sip, gossip, linger, in local decorum.

*****

There is protocol in this business of serving and tasting tea. It varies slightly from server to server, but more or less everyone abides by certain rules. The dried leaves are always handled with wooden, bamboo, or ceramic scoops (metal can taint the taste). Water is boiled to 100 degrees Celsius, utensils are doused, leaves are rinsed and rinsed again. The tea is never left long to steep in the pot.

The owner of Ming Yong Tea Factory sets a pot of water on a tabletop tray with a built-in burner. She scoops a spoonful of oolong into a clay serving pot. When the water boils, she rinses a set of tasting cups, then fills the pot and immediately dumps the water. The first pour is never to drink, only to "clean glass, clean tea," she explains. In a perfect mirror of the town's mingled cultures, our server goes by alternate names: Phantipa in Thai and Lin in Chinese.

She pours a second round of water over the leaves, then immediately transfers the tea to small, elongated cups for tasting—but not yet. A second, round cup is placed upside down over each vessel containing the tea. We allow them to sit a moment before flipping the ensembles. As all the locals instruct, we roll the elongated cups in our hands and lift them to our noses to absorb their fragrance. Then we place the hot cup on our eyes, as residents tell us it awakens one's vision.

Next, of course, we sip the tea. We taste an oolong infused with local herbs that smell of rice. We taste another oolong, #12, which offers a floral bouquet and a hint of bitterness at the back of the tongue. Oolong #17, by contrast, tastes and smells flowery throughout.

Though other varieties are grown, Mae Salong is known for its oolong tea, which, in terms of fermentation, falls between black (fully oxidized) and green (not oxidized at all). Dozens of shops sell oodles of oolongs, each imparting distinct characteristics that reflect the land, the water, the way the tea is grown and picked and dried. "My factory makes nineteen different teas," Lin says: each has its own fragrance, shape, and body.

A large factory room next door is abuzz with workers in motion. Women sort through mini-mountains of tea, removing stems from each pile of dried leaves spread across tarps on the floor. Another area houses freshly picked green leaves, supple to the touch. The entire room smells of sun tea on a summer day. Dryers growl and rumble as men load leaves onto a giant conveyor belt that switchbacks through the machines, coming out the bottom in streams of warm, crispy, dry leaves.

Across the street, at the Yeng Hong Factory, workers make giant cannonballs of leaves that are wrapped in cloth and rotated beneath a machine that spins the balls and presses them hard, bruising the leaves to begin fermentation. This continues for several minutes until an employee unravels the balls and dumps the tea into another spinning machine, which ultimately drops the leaves onto the ground for another worker to sort and sift.

*****

Some of Mae Salong's factories and plantations are little family-run affairs while others, such as the 101 Tea Plantation, lord over the landscape from sprawling hilltop perches. The 101 Visitor Center is equipped to handle tasters by the busload, with ample room to sample and buy.

And there is a lot to buy—pots, boilers, strainers, tongs, kitchen magnets, hundreds of cups, full tea sets, knickknacks, and bins and bags and bundles of tea. The walls are decked in photos and signs in Thai describing the necessary steps to process tea. First, the youngest growth is plucked from the plants. The leaves are "withered" in sunlight for ten minutes, then stacked in bamboo trays for winnowing. They're sorted, fermented, fired, rolled, spread, covered in white cloth, bound, kneaded, and dried.

Out on the sloping fields, nineteen workers weave their way through the rows, picking weeds and digging little holes for fertilizer pellets. It's a multicultural field bearing the distinctive dress of tribal villagers who live throughout this hilly region.

"Mingalaba!" A worker with a goatee greets us in Burmese. "We're all from Myanmar." Their homeland lies just a few miles west, a few days' stiff walking through this mountainous neck of the woods. Thailand's upland fields and farms are sprinkled with Burmese workers seeking jobs and opportunities that don't exist at home.

A woman picks a clump of pennywort growing among the tea plants. "You can eat," she says. "Delicious!" Here and there, the women stuff their sacks with the tea plantation's weeds—edible herbs they take home for dinner.

*****

This is my first up-close encounter with the region's tea—but it's not my first trip to Mae Salong. I initially visit these striking hills eighteen months earlier with a small group of Asian journalists who come to interview General Lue Ye-tein. It's cold that day, in the early November rain, and General Lue wears a heavy jacket with a furry collar. He greets us in his parlor, serving little cups of magnificent peach-fragrant tea. The general, in his early nineties, sports a silvery patch of hair and wiry tufts of eyebrows. He speaks with utter clarity, recalling his fellow soldiers' days in Yunnan, then Burma, then Thailand. "Before I was a soldier, I was just staying in the countryside in Yunnan," he says. "The Japanese invaded China so I had to become a soldier to protect China."

He ran away from home, to train in Nanjing. "I didn't want my parents to know," he says. "I had no money in my pocket." He walked many long hours, for days. "At that time my shoes were woven from grass. I could walk many kilometers."

That was the existence General Lue knew for decades. "My whole life was always walking and climbing mountains and carrying guns. Every day was exercise." War was life; it defined him in most every way. He has never wanted to return to the land that took his father, mother, and brother. "They were just all killed and thrown away."

His life, now, is firmly planted in the hills that grow this tea we drink from steaming little glasses. War is long gone; so is the opium trade—a subject he does not discuss. The general has moved on, happy to have found peace and a new prosperity for his people. "I'm not a soldier anymore," he says. "That's all history."

Chinese clay teapots for sale and use at a tea house in Mae Salong, Thailand. The town is home to several thousand ethnic Chinese.

12. A Little Sip of Yunnan in Northern Thailand - 2008, 2010

Burmese laborers work in a tea factory in the Mae Salong valley of Thailand.

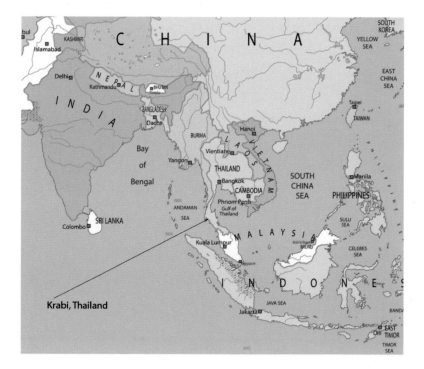

Krabi, Thailand

13. Eating My Way through Krabi - 2009

I feel the silence even before I taste the salt-thick air. It's the absence of noise, in a land flush with ruckus, that hits me first.

"So, what do you expect?" Mr. Bee asks. "Maybe quiet?"

He fetches the key to my private seaside bungalow and describes the local tempo. "Around here, there is nothing."

Here is Had Yao beach, a lone stretch of shell-cluttered sand along the Andaman Coast used sparingly by Muslim fishermen, who were the area's sole residents until a few upscale resorts opened their doors. It's still quiet, still full of nothing. Limestone karsts flank the horizon. They tell a phenomenal geological story of the collision between the Indian Subcontinent and Eurasia some 50 million years ago. That massive tectonic upheaval wrought crags and caves that form southern Thailand's landscape today. Harness-clad travelers flock to Krabi with ropes and carabiners and a yen to climb. I come instead for sea and sand, and food that has fed up to forty thousand years of people.

Most visitors never see beyond the area's few popular beaches, but this province spreads across ancient rainforests and unruffled shores. I take a walk. The clouds, the sea, the sand all shimmer in the same slate gray. A family loads a Styrofoam cooler with little fish and crabs. Villagers graze the water, chest-deep in waves. Dinner is nigh.

I love the hour when sunlight turns to butter cream. Employees prepare the evening tables, light glinting off pink-shirted backs. Sometimes the setting surpasses the menu—eight modest tables in the sand, a mild breeze, flickering candles, and flapping palms. It's one of those tropical nights when the temperature of skin and air harmonize as though two notes to a consonant song. I order a whole red snapper with a bed of crispy fried garlic and a sprinkle of black pepper. My seafood salad comes with a tangy lime sauce atop perfectly squeaky squid rings, celery leaves, onion, and red bell pepper. Nothing extraordinary, but everything lovely.

*****

Extraordinary lies up the road several miles, past rubber trees and oil palms, in a smattering of village cafes with stainless steel bins and recipes made to feed lunch crowds. No signs, just a shack with plastic chairs and collapsible tables. No menu, just a finger point and a nod to the vendors. The women behind these tables wear simple knit hats denoting their religion, Islam, which is an attribute that distinguishes this region's food and customs. Wander a beach at sunset, and you'll hear the Muslim call to prayer. Walk the streets, and you'll meet more goats than dogs. Cultural roots tend toward Malaysia, and kitchen habits hail from India.

I stop at a stall beside a neighborhood market, where I order gaeng som, a classic southern fish curry, hot and sour, as vivid as pumpkin; and a dollop of sweet-savory roasted coconut with lemongrass and curry. It's a spice combination that places me somewhere in the hills of Sri Lanka. Fresh cucumber slices, raw cabbage, and a bitter, pungent leaf accompany my lunch. "Pah ohm," a couple of fellow diners say in unison. They roll the supple leaf between their fingers, sniff it, then wrap it around a bite of coconut for an even keel of salty, bitter, sweet.

Farther up the road, in heart of Krabi Town, I find sidewalk food beside the entrance to a dermatology clinic. A waiting patient sees me eyeing the offerings, and she insists on helping me choose. "Papaya," she says, then wrinkles her nose. "Oooh, but spicy." Locals almost always assume the heat will offend a foreigner.

"Mai pen rai," I say. No problem.

"Then give her the sauce!" she instructs the vendor. Spicy lemongrass and kaffir lime permeate tender, thick slices of papaya and tiny shrimp in a butternut squash-colored curry. I nod toward a pyramid-shaped package and ask what's inside.

"Hor mok. Very delicious. You should try."

She's right. If fish had the seasoning of Italian sausage and the consistency of mousse—this would be it, steamed in a banana-leaf packet. I alternate between bites of fish and spoonfuls of curry.

"Can you eat?" my friend asks, still concerned for the well-being of my tongue.

"Yes!" I assure her.

She grins, then disappears to make a phone call, returning a moment later, faintly frantic.

"I'm sorry," she says. "This one we call green papaya." It's unripe, slightly sour, and has a different name in Thai than the sweet, ripe coral papaya eaten as fruit. Unsure she had told me the right name, she called her teacher who, she proudly notes, studied English at Bangkok's prestigious Chulalongkorn University. "Very famous," she says.

*****

Due west another dozen miles, along a hectic highway, a couple of women guard an array of pots—yellow fish curry, spicy beef curry, yellow beef curry, chicken bamboo curry, sweet peanut curry, green chicken curry, red squid chile, spicy fish soup, and spicy yellow crab. It's a do-it-yourself sort of joint. I ladle the crab over a muddle of rice noodles, then sit at a long picnic table with baskets of herbs—cilantro, sweet basil, lotuslike greens, and a variety of bitter leaves. A proper bowl of kanom jeen requires a bit of this, a bit of that, plus bean sprouts, wing beans, long beans, pea eggplants, sweet pickled peppers, savory pickled greens, dried anchovies, and coconut-cream spinach—all lined up in little dishes. Everything goes into the bowl for a hot-spicy-sweet-sour-bitter-salty-fishy zinger of a mouthful, smacking of lemongrass.

*****

A mouthful takes me back a year in time, to the trip that sold me on Krabi. That time, I found a twenty-dollar gem of a bungalow five feet from high tide, and a laid-back staff that went home at night, leaving me to my own devices. By day, I kayaked for hours through intermittent rains, paddling alongside limestone cliffs and hidden beaches as sea eagles, kingfishers, and monitor lizards scoped the waters for dinner.

This little paradise sits on a primeval crossroads linking Southeast Asia and the rest of the world. Bead mounds in a place called Klong Thom depict early trade routes connecting Thailand to the Middle East, China and India, Greece and Rome. Prehistoric foragers camped nearby during the Late Pleistocene thirty-seven thousand years ago. These ancient families settled here for the abundance of food, writes Thom Henley, an environmentalist and author of a naturalist's guide to the area. "There's an old saying that when the tide goes out the table is set." Today's beachcombers resemble a scene from ages past, with hands and feet probing for fish and clams, crabs and cockles.

Henley built my $20-a-night bungalow in a rustic resort named the Dawn of Happiness. I miss it, so I return. There, I sleep with windows wide, mosquito net tucked; the tide arrives in a rush at night, followed by screaming cicadas. Then birds, lush with song, greeting the dawn. By 9 a.m., the sea lies placid, gentle, like a silk sheet beneath the breakfast sun.

Around the bend is a 75-million-year-old cemetery of mollusks preserved in layered beds. From a distance, the beach appears littered with concrete slabs. Up close, I find clusters of fossils covered in tiny live creatures that scurry among the tidal knuckles between sea and land. They scatter as I approach, swift little things that look like shrimp mixed with cockroach genes.

But I'm equally interested in the hill above this beach, which supports a few little stalls selling fried chicken and Muslim curries. I approach in a midday lull as many locals take their siestas. But I point to a bin and immediately rouse a swarm of women. "Himaphan!" they shout. "Cashew! Eat! Eat!"

It's not the nut I find in my curry with salted fish—it's the cashew apple. A vendor ducks into her kitchen and returns with a bowl of freshly cut fruits, pale yellow. She sprinkles them with sugar. They're juicy, with a guavalike flavor and an endnote that sucks my mouth of all moisture. The women show me a specimen plucked from a tree. "Here's the flower. Here's the fruit," they explain. A curious thing: the apple sits atop the nut, which resembles a lima bean in its early stages. As it grows, the apple swells—until it's picked and sliced and curried by enterprising cooks of Krabi.

*****

A few days later I'm on my way to Khao Phanom Bencha National Park when my driver, Kuan, eyes a Sunday market. "Do you want to buy something to eat?" He stops the car, knowing little of the danger in his question. This could take hours. I wander past bright umbrellas shading tables stacked with fruits and vegetables, sweets and fish, meats and shells. I buy a deep-fried disc of tempura-battered shrimp and herbs. Eventually, Kuan appears and suggests we get back on the road. I ask him about the herbs and he chuckles. "Local leaf," he says. "We call it lep krut." It's bitter on its own but pleasant amid the greasy, crunchy shrimp, shell and all.

I also buy a bag of nuts with dark casings, which Kuan calls nieng. The nutmeat is juicy but it puckers the mouth. It stinks like sator, slightly sulphuric, but the end result should evoke pleasant aromas.

"When you go to the toilet, good smell," Kuan tells me in all seriousness. I consider buying a year's supply for Jerry.

When I settle into a bungalow on the edge of Phanom Bencha, I meet another face of Krabi. I see, from the perch of my porch, sunlight streaming down a limestone cliff that disappears upstream in a tangle of jungle. The highest mountain in Krabi towers over these primordial forests, 4,429 feet above. This landscape houses hundreds of bird and mammal species, many of them rare and endangered.

I enter that forest, skirting limestone formations with fantastical faces, as though Salvador Dalí worked here with a chisel. The forest has eyes, I am sure. I feel them on my neck and back.

I really do see the eerie eyes later in my bungalow when I discover a green snake on the bathroom wall. A viper, I'm fairly certain. It takes half an hour at slow slither for the serpent to exit through the slats between inside and outside.

Later, when I tell Son, the manager, about the snake, he smiles. "It's OK, it won't harm you." Snakes like to eat the resident geckos. My visitor was just going about its age-old business of big guys eating little guys in a system that has sustained the local food chain for millennia.

I, on the other hand, go back to the age-old human business of indulging in delightful fish sausage, cockle curry, and the most luscious whole crab on a bed of cilantro, lemongrass, shallots, chile, and lime.

A family catches fish in the Andaman Sea in Krabi, Thailand at sunset.

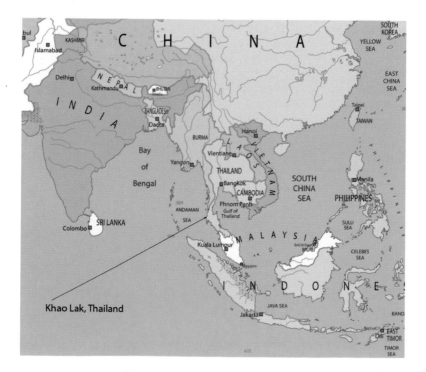

Khao Lak, Thailand

14. After the Waves - 2005

On December 26, 2004, an early morning earthquake rumbled the Indian Ocean off the coast of Indonesia. It triggered a tsunami that killed an estimated 275,000 people in eleven countries. Jerry and I were living in northern Thailand at the time, and we flew to the southern island of Phuket to cover the disaster for publications around the world. But as often happens during tragedies and war, another story develops around the journalist. That story seldom makes it to print. Below are my reactions reporting on one of the deadliest natural disasters in history.

I can't kill the stench, can't stand the reek of my clothes. I smell of rot, like the bloated corpses that lie in heaps at Wat Bang Muang on the edge of Khao Lak in southern Thailand. Death smothers the temple and eats through its shimmer.

Some of the victims are covered, hundreds are not. They don't look real, faces so puffed, tongues extended, bellies distended, breasts and penises erect. I see a child with maggots in the gut, a woman with a gash in the breast. Dry ice clouds swirl in eerie loops.

Workers tiptoe through these morbid avenues yelling "falang" when they identify a foreign corpse—it's no longer easy to do. Shell-shocked survivors scrutinize the piles. The bodies are no longer people. They are not humans, no life, nothing—absolutely nothing—left. Ashes to ashes, dust to dust, they are returning to the same Mother Nature that killed them.

This is Khao Lak, January 2005. On Christmas Day, thousands made merry on the beachfronts of southern Thailand, sunning and sailing and smiling for cameras, with the backdrop of bliss all around. The next day, everything changed. Death gushed through the door and broke it down.

*****

"If you do not see the reality, you will never understand what happened here," an Austrian volunteer named Walter Dreier tells me. His vacation has turned into a search-and-rescue mission. For days, he picks through rubble, looking for Austrians buried in sand. He finds identification papers for two people, no more.

It was nature, unbiased, invoking random selection, which killed a quarter million people. Pictures and words alone don't fully convey the scene. They don't translate smells or sounds or the overwhelming clench of desperation.

The sewers in town stink of death. I step over a manhole and I smell the temple; I smell my clothes, my hair, my bag—all over again.

I smell sad irony, too: The airport is warm and flowery, like paradise, like it should be. But the tarmac is stacked with coffins.

I hear calm waters lapping against placid shores. A red sun slips over a docile ocean, as stunning a view as ever. But strips of metal dangle from a ceiling, creaking in a creepy wind, as bulldozers crush their way through mountains of rubble. In some spared spots, little lizards rustle through lush vegetation. In others, nothing green remains. We wake one morning to helicopters thundering round and round; the drone of disaster.

I taste grief in sweet tangerines and greasy fried chicken, offered freely by hundreds of men and women toiling over bubbling woks. They've volunteered to feed the workers and journalists who have flooded this island. The cooks are happy to give but heartbroken for the reasons why.

I walk one night, alone, along the beach in Patong. It's a black cavity of nothing—nothing of what was here before. Think of Waikiki, snuffed of life. Bricks are stacked to be made into sidewalks again. The road is open, the debris mostly cleared to the sides. But no lights, no people, not even dogs. Step two blocks inland and the beer flows, the music thumps, in near-empty bars. Nearly all the customers are gone—either gone home or gone completely/washed away.

On Khao Lak beach, the waves pulverized everything, turning high-end resorts into rubbish. Everything is where it shouldn't be. Doors and windows litter the ground. An overturned truck rests in a hotel lobby. Electric wires lay in ditches. Concrete posts are snapped in half. A tree sprouts from the broken windshield of a vehicle stuck in mud.

Rescue workers pick through it all, meticulous work by hand, down in the sand. A man from Singapore digs through broken wood and concrete, pawing carefully, sniffing for the telltale smell of human remains. He is momentarily drawn to a curious spot, but his boss tells him never mind—it's only the odor of rotten fish.

Up the beach a bit, Jerry and I watch a Korean team going through similar motions. They find a backpack and spill its contents: a wallet, a cell phone, medications, lipstick. It belonged to a woman, that's all they can discern. The team has found eleven bodies and one leg in five days. The workers doubt they'll find more. They're moving north, where the tsunami wiped out an entire fishing village.

Evidence of the missing surfaces in tattered bits—a photocopy of Toth Ildiko's Hungarian passport, a March 1 Turkish Airlines boarding pass from Bangkok to Istanbul in Oliver Gutzke's name.

Most unnerving are the third-floor rooms of a Khao Lak resort, left as they were that morning. Jerry and I climb the dirty stairs. We see what life was like just moments before, as though we're traipsing through time. We find an open tin of mackerel, a glass of grape juice, John Grisham at the bedside. The next room over has crayons and dolls spread across a table. On the floor sits a survey asking "the opinions of international tourists toward Khao Lak."

In another room, we try to guess the course of events: A female occupant went swimming, and lived. She ran to the room, kicked in the door, grabbed a few items, and fled. She left little spots of blood on the bed.

We come to know something of the missing. One family had kids, one guest had a cold. Someone loved tea, another liked silk, someone else took expensive care of her hair and skin. One room has a cardboard Christmas tree in a corner.

Every room harbors a little freeze-frame of life before it vanished.

When people need more answers, they visit "the wall," an hour away in Phuket town. It's a sobering corridor of photos and fliers and phone numbers, lists of dead and injured, places last seen and pleas for help, all taped to dozens of blackboards in a parking lot. Workers here answer the phones twenty-four hours a day. A young woman named So Pida fetches a list of names and the resorts where missing people stayed. Nearly all of the addresses are the same: Khao Lak, Khao Lak, Khao Lak. "We work all day, all night," she says. "We cannot sleep."

I write about So Pida, the wall, the bodies at Bang Muang. I write many paragraphs, and the images stick in my head and my gut.

I drink a beer and my thoughts muddle. It's the same for Walter, the Austrian volunteer. After five days, he removes his mask and takes a break. He can't go back to those dreadful beaches, he says. "Last night I thought, 'I have to go out, I have to drink some beers.'" But he couldn't drown himself in an alcoholic elixir.

"It didn't work."

He can't shake the images, so he changes his mind and vows to search through sand again. "I have to," he tells me, with tiny tears misting his eyes.

And I have to look away. My eyes are as blurred as his.

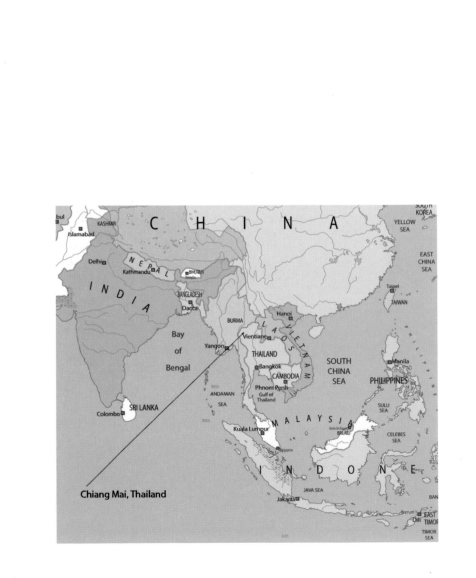

Chiang Mai, Thailand

15. Conversations with Exiles - 2003

"I am in exile," he tells us. Two years earlier, at the age of nineteen, he traveled on foot through the mountains of northern Burma and escaped to India. Of course it was scary and dangerous. But it was necessary. He's a journalist. He has lived in India for two years and now cannot contact his family back home—because they know. The Burmese military knows he has fled. There are thousands of Burmese exiles in India. If his family receives a letter from India, the authorities will grow suspicious. So instead, he mails a letter from Cambodia and signs it with a false name.

Phnom Penh is where we meet, where I am introduced to Burma. The young man is here with colleagues from Cambodia, Vietnam, and Laos through an internationally funded journalism program. The program's managers have organized an afternoon party. So I sit and chat with a few of the Burmese on dewy green grass. Another young reporter lives in exile in Chiang Mai, in northern Thailand, where he runs a Burmese newspaper; and a third works for a magazine in Rangoon. Unlike the others, he will return home to Burma when this project finishes. He travels on a legal passport with his true name. The others have fake IDs.

The man from Rangoon calls himself a laborer because, "if I ask for a journalist's passport, they never give to me." He says many people buy fake Burmese passports from a broker who charges about four hundred dollars. But those passports only take you so far, for so long.

The Chiang Mai man says he can never return to Burma. The Burmese government knows what he does in Thailand—he prints stories on human rights abuses, landmines, and illegal logging committed by the Burmese government; all issues that could never be covered in Burma. But he doesn't fear retaliation from the Burmese, not in Chiang Mai. They'd have to firebomb his office, he says, and he doesn't think that will happen. Instead, he fears the Thais. They're in cahoots, working with the junta, he says. Still, he is safer in Thailand than at home.

"We are lucky Burma has such a porous border with India, and such a porous border with Thailand," the one from India says. He envies our ability to travel. "If my parents knew you went around the world, they would be very surprised." This is a luxury that Burmese writers do not have. "In my country, all the writers are poor. All of them." We tell him by U.S. standards, we are poor as well, and that journalists have a bad name in our country—a concept that stuns him. In Burma, he says, journalists struggle to eat. He talks of a writer walking the streets, always walking because he has no money for transportation. Year after year, he wears the same tattered clothes and totes the same rucksack over his shoulder. Twenty years, forty years—nothing changes. But that writer is respected. "In my country, all people believe the writers," the exile says. What they do is essential to "the movement." Many writers go to jail. Some of them die there.

The three young men talk about writers still in jail after fifty-two years. "Fifty-two years!" they repeat for emphasis. They tell us about a prison, visible from the road to the popular mountaintop temple tourist spot, the Golden Rock featured in National Geographic. From the road, it's possible to see prisoners cutting rock, building roads by hand. They make half of a cent a day. "They get no food," the Chiang Mai man says.

"They are like animals," all three agree.

These young men are hungry for someone to tell the stories they can't. They starve for freedom. The man from India wants me to write about education. In 1998, they tell us, the Burmese government divided the universities geographically into four disparate campuses so students could never unite and revolt. The Chiang Mai man draws a map, showing the rivers that separate his country's students.

The Rangoon man tells us he would like to stay in touch, but when he returns home, he will not be able to use Hotmail or Yahoo—both blocked. So he gives us an alternate address where we can reach him at his magazine.

I suddenly have a sharp pang of inadequacy. I was invited to speak to their class about freelance journalism. But I realize these students are doing all the teaching.

As the afternoon draws on and the mingling continues, I talk with an American journalism trainer who has traveled to Burma. It's so different, she says. The people are educated, despite the government. The students are sharp. They want to discuss Dickens and Kerouac. She loves it.

*****

One night later that week, Jerry and I visit the Burmese journalists at the rented house they share. The dim, tile-covered room fills with intense words and thick smoke as the guys pluck cigarettes from a single red pack. They flick a lighter, tap their feet with nervous energy, and speak with their hands.

Jerry asks the guys about the Burmese military—they must have friends from childhood who are soldiers now. And they do. "This is not my path," the man from India says. But people choose that route for money and security, a chance to get ahead.

Are they still friends? I ask.

"No," he says. "That is their choice."

Yet for all these men have seen and suffered, they remain remarkably optimistic. They think the Burmese government is unsustainable and they think its leaders realize they must one day change. The change won't be instantaneous or perfect, they say. But democracy is coming. They are sure of it.

*****

Just a few months later, we're living in Chiang Mai. Maung, the Burmese journalist we met in Cambodia, invites us to his newsroom. It's a rambling house he shares with his workmates.

We arrive and Maung is pounding red chile with a mortar and pestle. He cooks for the staff. "Yeah, today is my duty." Everyone takes a turn in the kitchen. Maung fries the chile in oil, adds a little water, chopped chicken, and shallot.

The newsroom fills with the fire of hot curry. Maung wears a white T-shirt and dark plaid longyi. A pile of chile stems surrounds his bare feet on the wooden floor. He smokes a Burmese cheroot with a Thai label covering the Burmese label. "This comes from the border," he says, that theoretical line through the jungle that hard-pressed villagers and dissidents risk their lives to cross.

The journalists eat before they work; a full belly is the first step toward a free Burmese press. "In Burma I never cooked," Maung says. "My mother insisted I work."

Maung has a helper, Pount, who shuffles between the kitchen and newsroom. She's the assistant editor's wife, who also serves as the paper's accountant. When she finishes in the kitchen, she sits on the hard living room floor and proofs pages with a green marker, stroking a fat calico cat about to burst with kittens.

Life and work converge in these rooms, in seamless stride. A green lighter sits on the floor beside a metal film canister filled with cheroots. Another editor named Zin sprawls across a mat with an English-Burmese dictionary open to the word "purity." He's editing an English-language story on tennis at the Asian Games and translating the article into Burmese. The walls around him are adorned in cheat sheets that show Burmese/English keyboard functions. It's 5:10 p.m. on a Sunday, but this staff steps to a nontraditional beat. They work odd hours scattered across the calendar.

A marker board notes the week's news. September 16: two are sentenced to seven years imprisonment and held in Insein Prison (aptly pronounced "insane"). Ne Win's relatives are sentenced to death by hanging. The staff discusses the news, speaking in Burmese with low, guttural Bs and Ws and Os rolling around in their mouths like marbles.

A subeditor named Win enters the room with freshly washed hair, long and damp. "We are waiting," Maung says. They expect a story soon on a new border crossing between Thailand and Burma, set to open in a day or two. "But my deadline is today." So the staff will print extra pages in an insert carrying the latest news. Meanwhile, yet another editor, named Kyaw, searches for photos to accompany the articles. Some reporters shoot and send their photos by e-mail, he says, "and also we download from the Internet and we scan it from The Nation or the Bangkok Post—whatever we can get." They use PageMaker on locally made computers that have been cobbled together from an assortment of brands and parts. They paid 20,000 baht each ($463 in the day) for four computers with keyboards and monitors. "Very cheap," Kyaw says.

A Burmese reporter for an international wire service is here visiting, and he is eager to share his life story. He's forty-two years old; he fled Burma—and his family—fourteen years earlier after the 1988 student uprising in which at least three thousand people were killed. "My son was born in 1989, shortly after the crisis," he says. "So I did not meet my son until he was seven. But now it is better. I can go to visit them one time each year." He returns home during the annual water festival, which marks the Burmese New Year each April. He says he's safe to fly into Rangoon as long as he conducts no journalistic business. But the border, not far from Chiang Mai, he cannot cross. "It's dangerous." For him, and for all journalists like him

We talk while Maung spell-checks a story on Chinese aid for telecommunications projects in Burma's northeastern Shan State. Digital phone service, he says. Click, click, click—we watch as he pounds the keyboard speedily making circular Burmese characters move on screen. Then he gets up abruptly to serve hot, sugary, creamy coffee to everyone in the room.

The paper also has an in-house illustrator. "When I was in Burma, I never drew the cartoons," he says. Too political. He worked with almost everyone in this room at one point in Burma before sneaking across the border at Mae Sot, a town on the Thai side of the border that serves as a hub for migrants, traders, and refugees. "I hid for almost four months before that," he says. "All of my family stays in Burma." He rarely hears from them. "They don't want to contact me." It's too dangerous. But he dreams of someday taking his work home. "I hope."

*****

Win thinks the paper is succeeding; its circulation has hit one thousand. "That is like a green light for us," he says. To satisfy a growing readership, they've added pages and increased space for arts and entertainment. "I hear from our distributor," he says, "people want to see more entertainment photos, especially actors and actresses in Burma." A colleague complained to him: Why so much entertainment? But Win understands his readers. The Burmese in Chiang Mai are constantly faced with the perils of war and disorder. "Their lives cannot be serious all of the time," he says. "So we have to balance."

The room is noisy with tapping keyboards and flicking lighters. After dark, it's all fluorescence and computer light. A pot of ramen sits waiting while Maung chatters on the phone, something about Kofi Annan.

Win tells us we should return at 1 p.m. Tuesday. They'll be preparing for the distributor to deliver the paper to the night bazaar, where it is sold to Chiang Mai's Burmese underground. The distributor, he says, is a "secret agent." Many of the night bazaar's four hundred workers are Burmese migrants, "but they all pretend they are Thai." The paper, he says, "they take and read at home." It would be dangerous to do so in public. There are tourist police with careful eyes. Their paper is not found on the stands. People who buy it know where it is, they know who sells it, and they know who is Burmese faking a Thai face.

As we continue to talk, Maung contemplates his editorial for the evening. He planned to write about a UN delegate headed to Burma, urging him to investigate human rights abuses and claims that the Burmese military has raped women in Shan State. But the UN envoy postponed the trip, which means Maung must come up with something else.

I ask Maung if he thinks he's a good editor, and he shakes his head. "I don't think so," he says. "Because this is a small paper. I have no experience working with a lot of people. But I must try. A good editor has many, many problems and many, many deadlines." He struggles with ideals. "Especially to keep the highest journalistic ethic. And the writing style. And the professional way. In Burma, this has been lost a long time ago. We must fight again." He also has the drive, the urge, to work as a freelance reporter. "I love to go to the outside. I love to travel. I love to meet with people." But for now, he cannot.

*****

We return, as asked, on Tuesday afternoon. The paper is finished, it looks good. "We will take to the post office," Win says, "and just one or two days they will arrive for our subscribers." It's mailed to readers across Thailand in Bangkok, Mae Sai, Mae Sot, Kanchanaburi, and Nonthaburi.

Maung enters the room in a longyi, no shirt. He's carrying a drenched, clean puppy named Ringo and takes the dog outside to dry. A young woman stamps each paper with a price in blue ink: 10 baht (23 cents). She's surrounded by piles of papers, brown wrapping, string, scissors, and packing tape. One hundred subscriptions, mostly exiles.

This week's edition contains coverage of political prisoners, press freedom, migrant workers in Mae Sot, Canadian demands for the downfall of the Burmese regime, former President Jimmy Carter winning the Nobel Peace Prize, South Americans protesting Columbus Day, an analysis of businesses withdrawn from Burma, the benefits of lemon juice for a healthy pregnancy, Pakistan missile testing, Xanana Gusmao gaining money from UNESCO, nightclub workers in Indonesia, Madonna's problems with a newly built fence, the public's hopes for a Tom Cruise-Nicole Kidman reunion, Manchester United, Spanish bullfighting, and golf. In the end, Maung has focused his editorial on the Burmese economy: he argues that the international community should give the generals no money.

Maung leaves the room momentarily, then returns—dressed and smoking. He starts addressing packages of papers for the mail.

Five staff members sit around the room, paging through papers, laughing, and sipping small glasses of weak milky coffee. Pount tells me she studied international relations in Rangoon, but education is very bad there. "Burmese students cannot study at the library or on the Internet. Only textbooks." It costs about 500 kyat (50 cents) a day to cover the teachers' tea and supplemental costs. Many students cannot afford those fees. "It's very difficult to go to school," she says.

Maung looks rested, now that deadline has passed. "I'm very happy," he says. We spread the paper across the floor and critique design and style. He decides it looks much better than the typical paper in Burma. He shows me an example from Rangoon. It's tabloid size, eleven items on the front page, boxes and doglegs, convoluted layout and questionable content. Win points to the front page and calls it a government mouthpiece. Another page features the definition of police: Politeness, Obedience, Loyalty, Intelligence, Courage, Efficiency. In the back are the classifieds. "In Burma, people start to read the newspaper from the back," he says. "Never, never read the front news."

That's not the case with their own paper, Maung says.

I ask him if he thinks his colleagues in Burma do a good job. "That is difficult to say…many journalists are not very good because they do not know the rules of journalism," he says. "And also, they face a lot of challenges with the censorship board." Every paper, every article published in Burma must first pass the scrutiny of censors. Most Burmese journalists have no exposure to a free press. "Now I try to teach to the other writers and exiles," Maung says.

He learned nothing about journalism in Burma. "Nothing. I started learning about newspapers just three years ago…I was amazed to read a newspaper outside of Burma because before, I didn't see any real newspapers. I love to read the newspapers every day, every day, every day!" He thinks a moment. "We have lost a lot of journalism in Burma." He thinks many Burmese reporters misunderstand the purpose of journalism. "Some, they think newspapers only work to criticize politics. I say no, not only to criticize politics." The purpose of journalism is to inform the public and report without bias.

In 1999, Maung left Burma. The Bangkok Post was the first paper he remembers. I ask if he has ever seen The New Yorker, Harper's, The Atlantic. No—but he's very interested. "I have no experience with…" His voice trails and he turns to watch Ringo vomiting on the floor. "Oh my God! Yesterday she ate a lot…"

He runs off to comfort and massage the dog before returning for more serious talk on press freedom.

This young man is not just publishing a newspaper. He is building an ark of exile, and he's filling it with all of his trusted colleagues. Maung floats in the purgatory of Thailand, steering a ship adrift between imprisonment at home and freedom beyond his horizon.

*****

A few years later, Maung and his colleagues got word that the Thai government was cracking down on Burmese refugees in northern Thailand. Through UN help, they were resettled in other countries, and some of them now live scattered across the United States. They were given just a couple of weeks to prepare for that move and the start of a whole new life.

Right: A handful of exiled Burmese journalists work together to create a Burmese-language newspaper for the large Burmese community that works in Chiang Mai, Thailand. They work and live together in a house on the edge of Chiang Mai.

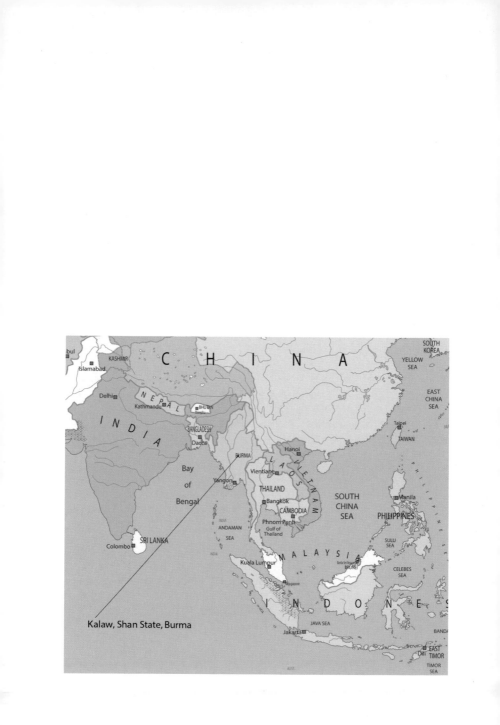

Kalaw, Shan State, Burma

16. Shan State Diary - 2002

Somehow, buses and trucks manage the route to Kalaw most every day. The main highway is a single crumbling lane with chewed-up shoulders that trace the snaking road, shooting between rocky ridges. Occasionally the trees part and the view opens, and from the bus window we gaze upon miles and miles of valley bottom, farther below us with each turn—undulating hills and far-off masses of steaming green. The road rises and the air grows cool. But the road offers no sympathy to big loads. Truck drivers honk at every blind bend, every fifty feet or so. They wait. They pull to the side and squeeze past each other like two fat men meeting in a doorway. Sometimes drivers leave their seats to direct other trucks safely around them. But other times, they do not.

This is why it takes twenty-three hours from Rangoon to Kalaw; three hours alone from the Mandalay turnoff, where the road grows smaller yet, and steeper. The journey begins with an hour parked on Rangoon's outskirts, while the driver fixes a broken fuel pump just a few miles from the bus station; plus another forty-five minutes on the roadside spent dousing the radiator with cool water; and all the time between 2:30 and 5 a.m. at a dingy truck stop who knows where, while several young men slowly repair a rear tire. We stop once more at six, and from my seat I see an early morning mist shrouding the highway and all the surrounding green fields. I hear the familiar clanking of tools, and the bus shakes as our navigators yank at this and that and every other part below. I have no idea what's wrong, but this particular repair takes half an hour.

Our expedition crosses towns with no motorcycles or cars. Trucks wheeze through, carrying goods to other destinations. But the locals amble along or ride a bicycle or ride in an oxcart. At night, there is virtually no electricity in the towns we pass. Shops and homes are lit by little candles surrounded in plastic. The occasional fluorescent light tied to a car battery illuminates a cigarette stall or cafe, but there is no karaoke, no screeching TV, no booming stereos or blinking lights. Though our drive parallels a series of high-tension power lines, none of the people beneath them have lights. The lines pass over green rice beside thatched shacks and people walk everywhere. For those on the ground, little has changed since Orwell lay his words to paper.

*****

The 5 p.m. sun glints off the gold-leaf wall across the street, setting the room ablaze. What look to be amber lightbulbs shimmering on every edge, above every carving, in every nook and cranny of that temple, on closer inspection are candles. This is the view to which I wake from my nap. It's a calming visual treat after that twenty-three-hour bus ride.

Tonight is the celebration of nine thousand lights, a ceremony following the end of Buddhist Lent when monks return to the social world after a season spent in contemplation inside their temples. And now: this reverie of light. Our guesthouse sits within view of a monastery's grounds, covered in a dozen or more stupas with tiny oil candles in minuscule ceramic holders climbing the whitewashed walls. Children come from all corners; adults and monks, too—clambering about the white structures, lighting more and more candles until the whole yard is awash in light. A city of lights. A dozen gleaming buildings against a starry sky with the shadows of worshippers dancing in the glow.

A pushy young man demands that Jerry take his portrait amid the gaiety. Then he insists two friends join him for the photograph. Soldiers. "Burmese Army," he chimes.

A man festooned in maroon approaches me. He says he used to run a trekking service but he closed the shop eleven months earlier and became a monk. He promised himself he would devote one year to the temple. He asks whether we have gone trekking yet, to meet the hilltribe villagers who populate the Shan State hills. "You should go," he urges. "It's very important for the tourist to see them in their traditional dress."

We sit among thumping drums and rumbling gongs, as men and women dance in traditional style. Nearby is a shriveled old monk covered in bright blankets and a maroon hat, so his body appears lost in a mound of cloth. But his little brown face peeks through, and people bow to his feet. My companion tells me that man is ninety-seven years old.

Behind all the light, the green glow of a mosque contrasts with this brilliant Buddhist fervor. It's a telling sign of the local medley—of people, cultures, histories, and daily lives. There are faces from the central highlands of Asia. There are others from the lowland Southeast. A Nepali woman runs an Everest restaurant. A local trekking guide comes from the Sino-Tibetan state known as Kayah. Another local guide is the son of a Pakistani tailor who moved here with the British Army.

The streets of Kalaw seem alive in the same way as the old quarter of Lhasa in Tibet. So many peoples on so many journeys through life. Up the road in Thaunggyi, those worlds merge in trade—gems, poppies, Chinese merchants, smugglers, warlords. Here, perhaps, there is some of the same. But this is an old hill station where, everyone tells us, foreigners have long enjoyed the respite from unrelenting heat. The streets are wide and absent of motorized traffic. Horse carriages gather at a local taxi stand. Feet provide the most commonly used transport, on vast roads and tidy sidewalks lined with the most beautiful array of flowers. All around: hills. Chilly breezes. Grasshoppers the size of one's hand. We're 5,250 feet high on the land.

*****

The 6 a.m. sun of Kalaw rises behind the pagoda in a pillow of mist. Once again, gold glimmers on a soft white background. Gold shrouded in down. This, too, is the view straight from my pillow.

I am amazed at the beauty of tormented lands.

We meet Mr. T. He's seventy-eight but looks sixty. For the past two years, he has run a little restaurant in Kalaw. He says he was born here and has seen Burma though the British, the Japanese, and the current military dictatorship, the Tatmadaw. When he learns we are Americans, he says that's very good. Ages ago, he had an American teacher, a Baptist missionary who left sometime after independence in 1948. Now, Mr. T says, the army occupies his old Baptist school.

Mr. T shares his opinions on the changing guards. The British? "Oh, very easy: no problem at all." The Japanese, however, were different. He remembers this area being bombed more than once, and the Japanese occupied this territory for four years. Those were not good years, he says.

And now?

We need not ask Mr. T because he offers his mind, unprompted. "Now it is peace. There are no problems except for the politic." He tells us repeatedly: "This country is not so bad. It's not like Indonesia. Indonesia has some terrorist problems." This, he says, he learns from watching the BBC: it is not allowed, though he's still able to tune in through satellite TV. He also reads articles in news magazines that tourists leave behind.

I ask whether he ever sees Time magazine.

"Noooo. We are not allowed." But he can read other things—on his own, in private. "I do not read in front of them," he says.

Them. The authorities.

We discuss a recent spate of bombings in Myawaddy, a southeast town near the Thai border. Mr. T has heard the place was shelled. We tell him Thai news has reported on several bombs found in parcels around town.

"That is different," Mr. T says. "Thailand is a democratic country and you can read the real thing." But then he adds that many democratic countries—such as India and Pakistan—suffer terrorist problems that Burma does not.

We mention a recent article in Time about al-Qaeda-linked terrorist groups training men on the Burma-Bangladesh border. This Mr. T does not believe. But then he concedes: he is not allowed to read uncensored news. "Anyway," he says, "we have peace, and that is good." Shan State, and Burma as a whole, is safe for tourists, he says. "You can go anywhere." There are many soldiers in town, he says. But when I ask whether they bother the locals he says, "No, no, nothing like that." And then our conversation shifts.

Mr. T tells us about his previous working life as a government administrator. He earned about three hundred kyat a month, a livable wage at the time. Since his retirement in 1978, he says, he has drawn a six-hundred-kyat monthly pension—hardly enough to sustain him now. He says it costs one thousand kyat a day, about a dollar, just to live. So he runs this restaurant.

Mr. T thinks poverty is the biggest problem, the biggest danger his country faces. But he thinks Burma could develop quickly with a little help, and perhaps a little reshuffling of priorities. He recently heard the government bought several MIG-29 fighter jets for defense. We heard them racing overhead when we were in Rangoon. Mr. T asks us how we think the government paid for them. "By hook or by crook," he says. "So much wasted money." Through proper investments, he thinks his country could prosper.

But jobs are hard to find. Many international companies have left because of human rights abuses. It does the people no good, he says. When companies leave, Burmese go jobless. People go hungry. They eat once a day. Things change, people change—like the weather.

Mr. T says in British times, this place was covered in acres of pines. But most of the trees are gone now—logged—and the air is warmer. Pipes no longer freeze in wintertime. Thin sheets of frost no longer cover the ground on cold mornings.

Yet he continues to defend this country he calls home. Compared with other governments, he says, his is not so bad. He leads us outside to a tangled vine of gourds, and he shows us the bulbous fruit. He wishes to give us seeds, a gift for us to plant at home. Sadly, I tell him, our government will not allow us to bring foreign seeds into our country.

So instead, he asks us to spread the word about his restaurant. On good days, he gets about fifteen customers. But "sometimes, not even one." He gives us his card. "Not so many Americans come here," he says. It's a cheery little place on a slope, on the edge of town, easy for any tourist to find.

*****

We visit a hilltop monastery just as the monks recite their afternoon prayers. They chant, imbuing the open room with song and peace, and I want to close my eyes. (Some monks do, snatching sweet moments of sleep.)

Outside, we meet a wrinkled old monk who leans against his window, beckoning conversation. He asks us to sign his guest book, to leave a postcard, to let him pray for us. He gives us oranges as gifts, then grasps our hands and counts along on his string of brown beads.

After prayers, the old monk shows us a booklet containing the prescriptions his doctor has ordered. Then he points to the record book, his official accounting of donations. We understand. We offer an FEC, the official government currency. He tells us his empty package of pills costs three hundred kyat for a refill—so we offer him that amount, too.

*****

We eat dinner at a local Shan restaurant: fritters served with a spicy salsa of peanuts, tomatoes, onions, garlic, and chiles. Soup with spinach and tomato slices in a fragrant stock with coriander and cinnamon. Chicken and tofu curry in a tomato sauce with garlic, onions, and lots of ginger. Side servings of plain rice, chile, slices of dried bean curd, fried water spinach, onion, and chile. Hot tea and flaming fried bananas for dessert.

It's a feast, eaten with gusto, sold for pennies.

*****

We rise, but the sun does not. The sky closes on Kalaw like a rain-spattered shutter. This does not bode well for the start of a three-day trek, but we find our guide, Ms. V, ready to go. She's wearing sneakers with a Chinese-style suit in thick indigo cotton and a rattan hat with a wide brim. Both she and her intrepid assistant, Mr. Z, have walking sticks in hand.

We stop first at the market to buy batteries and a few supplies; then we hike across town, past the railroad station, past children en route to school, past sopping wet riders on bicycles; past everyone and everything until the pavement peters out and becomes trail. There, we turn uphill, into a stand of wet trees.

Ms. V remembers when all the hills around Kalaw were covered in pines, like these. That was fifteen years earlier, before the government sold the trees to Japanese buyers. She remembers the men coming to Kalaw with big machines, chopping the forest in swift precision. "It has changed the weather, too," she says, echoing Mr. T. Europeans came to Kalaw for cool temperatures in times past. But the mercury rises now.

We climb steep hills and slog through thick, goopy mud. Ms. V tells us it's all government land, all around us. The Burmese people, the Shan, the Pa-O, the Danu—every ethnic group faces the same scenario. Farmers merely work their plots of land, which belong to the government. Villagers pay taxes on their crops. They pay the same price each season—rain or no, big harvest or none. "Sometimes it's very difficult for them," Ms. V says. In addition, each farmer must sell up to 30 percent of his crop to the government at a cut rate.

Ms. V comes from a multicultural family; her parents share five ethnicities between them. She speaks seven languages, which gives her good insights into the world around her. "I am a lucky girl," she says.

*****

It is only 9 a.m., but mist turns to droplets and we are wet with glistening skin: rain on the outside, sweat on the inside. But the view is a spectacle of color, a patchwork of fields—green mountain rice, yellow sesame, the snaking route of a slick red path. We slide our way up as buffalo herders come down. They are Danu, Ms. V says, and the animals don't like our scent. The big gray beasts lumber to the side, into the bushes to avoid our tread.

The Danu people came from China long ago, Ms. V says. The old folks still wear traditional short white shirts with black trousers or longyis, the ubiquitous Burmese checkered sarong. Like most tribes around here, the Danu are Buddhists. "Every full moon day and new moon day, they go to the monastery." Other days, they go to the fields. The villagers grow cauliflower, cabbage, garlic, and two types of rice. Twenty-five years earlier, Ms. V says, these people also grew poppies. But no more.

As we descend into a fecund valley, our mud path devolves into an oxcart road of hoofprints sunk six inches deep in the wet earth. We hop and jump and tumble. Jerry lands knee-deep in mud and loses a boot in the quickening sludge. This is a well-fertilized trail, and it all gets churned in the rain.

We arrive at a village home belonging to a sixty-five-year-old matriarch wearing the signature orange plaid headscarf of her people. She has a blazing fire in the center of her hut on stilts, and she welcomes us to its warmth. She blows through a bamboo tube to stoke the flames. Gourds steam above the fire.

"This rainy season there is a lot of rain, but we are happy because of the rice and vegetables," she says. "But some of the children go walking in it and they are ill—a lot of coughing."

I'm thrilled to speak with this woman. Jerry and I have hiked hundreds of miles across Southeast Asia, and it's remarkable how little we hear from the women we meet. The amount of time spent chatting with women is inversely proportional to the number of times we have had male guides. This time, it's different.

This time, our guide leads us first to the women of the house. Ms. V knows most of these villagers already, and they all greet her with glee. And they talk. We all talk—about husbands, kids, diapers, and farming. Meanwhile, Mr. Z works vigorously in the background preparing meals.

Our hostess tells us about her life, and the lives of her neighbors. She and her husband had ten children, but two died. Half live in this village, half in another. They're all married, and she has thirty or more grandchildren. "I cannot count."

Right now, the villagers are preparing to plant garlic, separating the cloves, she says. "In the next fifteen or sixteen days, we will harvest the fields, and after we will plant the garlic." She says this village has a government-run school with teachers from Kalaw. The children learn Burmese, English, and math—though no one goes to school during harvest time.

When she was young, she says, there was no school; neither did the houses have brick or bamboo. The village has changed and grown. "It started with six houses, then ten houses, now fifty," she says. "My grandsons are lucky because the living standards are higher." This village even has a TV.

"In Myanmar, we have two channels," Ms. V says. "One channel is from the government and the other channel is army. So same thing."

Our hostess says she will go to the Kalaw market in the morning with a load of soy beans, which sell for one hundred kyat a cup. I ask how much money her family makes in a year of farming, and the question sparks a conversation. She doesn't know. No idea. She never amasses money. She doesn't sell her rice in the market—only beans and other crops. She grows everything organically, using fertilizer from her cows. Her family eats very little meat; during the rainy season, they catch fish and dry it for consumption throughout the year. The mountain rice she serves us for lunch comes from the previous year's surplus. She sells the required amount of rice to the government for 25 percent of the market rate.

I ask our hostess what she thinks about the government.

"I never think about the government," she says. "Only harvest time."

She serves us fresh avocado with a pinch of sugar. Ms. V and Mr. Z give our hostess an envelope with a bit of money, a washcloth, and a bar of soap—a tradition "to wash away" any unintentional harm we bring or any misspoken words. And then we head down the trail toward another village.

*****

We continue through a rainbow of red dirt and green fields dotted with the stark white points of stupas. Ms. V says their presence is calming. "If we see the pagoda or stupa, we have to think of the five precepts," the Buddhist moral code of ethics calling for abstention from killing, stealing, sexual misconduct, hurtful speech, and intoxication.

We pass Pa-O women planting potatoes, their hoes thump thump thumping against the earth. Potatoes are a staple here, along with ginger, sesame, and peanuts. A couple of oxcarts atop the hill are loaded with potato sacks, which the villagers will take to market in the morning. It's a one-hour trek to the road, then a bumpy ride in the back of a pickup before reaching Kalaw.

Ms. V retrieves a package of multivitamins from her bag and hands them to the women. Everyone around here could use a vitamin or two.

Not much farther along the trail is a small village where we will spend the night. Our host is a seventy-four-year-old elder who spent nine years as village chief. It was a tough job, he says. He had to solve everyone's problems.

We talk about travel—this village gets a couple of foreigners every few months, but we are the first to visit this home. Last year, our host family visited Mandalay and the great old temples of Bagan. They went as pilgrims and stayed in a monastery. "I was happy," our host mother says. She experienced many things, such as heavy traffic on the city's busy pavement. "If we crossed the road, it was very exciting."

Three years before that, our host says, he accompanied several village men on a foot trek to the Thai border, in order to sell their cows. It took eighteen days, and in every village along the way, the men had to pay a tax to the authorities. The cow trade is part of the black market, he says. On the return, everyone contracted malaria. "It's not good business."

Our hosts tell us they had ten children, but one died at the age of sixteen. She suddenly, inexplicably, suffered a paralysis that lasted six months. The parents don't know what caused it—perhaps standing in wet paddies for several days during planting season, they guess. They took their daughter to the hospital in town, but the doctors could not save her.

*****

The family has an open fire that both warms the house and cooks the food. They ask if we cook like this, and I explain the concept of ovens, stoves, and microwaves. Ms. V has seen a microwave in Kalaw, but she has never used one. Our hosts don't know what it is, so we explain.

And then we talk about September 11; our hosts never heard the news. They are shocked to hear of all the deaths and equally intrigued to learn of buildings one hundred stories high and airplanes big enough to hold everyone they know. A neighbor joins our conversation, and she says sometimes their government flies helicopters very low overhead while she works in the mountains and fields. "Sometimes our government checks for the opium," Ms. V explains. The helicopters scare the woman; she certainly has no desire to try a 747.

We continue our conversation through a feast of curry with potato, eggplant, tomato, onion, garlic, and beef; peapods and onion, mustard leaf and ginger soup, green bean salad, two types of rice, fried prawn crackers, and oranges. Bellies full, we sleep that night on the hard floor of their wooden home, and we rise early for another day on the trail. Before we go, our hosts feed us heartily and invite us to come again; to stay longer and visit their fields. They cannot travel to our country, but we are welcome here—and they hope to meet us again in the next life.

✶✶✶✶✶

As we hike, we pass little crabapples on the trail. Ms. V says the villagers do not plant those trees; they grow naturally in several varieties. The wood is used for fires and the fruits are eaten in sweets and salads.

A few hours later, we're in the living room of a seventy-six-year-old widow who offers us lunch. Her daughter and granddaughter are here, as well as a neighbor friend. It's a perfect opportunity to talk about gender.

Is it better to be a Pa-O woman or man? I ask.

"A man," our hostess answers with conviction. "We don't have the same power. If we go to the monastery, the men can go near the monks." Women must keep their distance. "Only the men take care of monks. The women cannot," she says. "Also, we have to give birth to children, which is very difficult." All the women of the house agree: "Men are stronger."

Yet I watch these women, all wrapped in red scarves and bright orange head-cloths, with smiles beaming as they coo over a newborn baby, and I think: There is power and strength here in the bonds among women; I do not see the same bonds among men.

✶✶✶✶✶

That night, we stay in a big house belonging to a relatively wealthy Daun Dhu family. The husband is seventy, his wife thirty-seven, and they have three children.

Our dinner conversation covers tornadoes and earthquakes; Starbucks, Microsoft, McDonald's, and Nike—all unfamiliar to our hosts. The husband asks if we have tribes in our country, and this leads to a conversation about Native American genocide. We live worlds apart, but we share much. "When I was young," our host says, "my father told me all human beings come from one man and one woman. So we are the same. We come from different countries but we are the same." Then, as a side note, he adds: "Our skin is different. But I think that also depends on the weather."

✶✶✶✶✶

We wake to a New Moon Day, and we visit the local monastery—all wood, all smoke, with two old monks sitting beside a fire burning in a wok. The air is damp and chilled. The ceiling drips, and the water runs through a hole in the floor (Buddhist solution to a leak?). As we chat with the monks, they sit on a raised platform twelve feet from V and me. As our female companions noted the previous day, a distance is required between monks and the other gender.

The elder monk here is ninety; he shaved his head and donned the robe at eighteen. A portrait of his younger self, at seventy-eight, presides over the big, airy chamber of this temple. Nine men sit around us now; they come from villages near and far. Each spends two days working and sleeping in the temple. It's a responsibility that no upstanding villager shirks.

As we leave the monastery, I ask Ms. V whether locals ever grow up and decide not to be Buddhist. She chuckles. "Noooooo!" Devotion is never questioned. It's a given. This is a region of many givens for many people. The nine-year-old daughter in one of our homestays rises at 4 a.m. to light the candles in a little Buddhist shrine that hangs above our sleeping heads. She places an offering plate on the altar and bows to say her prayers. And then she prepares pumpkin soup for our breakfast. It's her duty. It's her given.

*****

Later that day, we stumble into Kalaw with tired feet and filthy clothes. For the first long stretch in three days, the clouds break. The rain disappears just as our hiking ends. We learn, now, that the entire course of our trek has stretched through "restricted areas," legally off-limits to foreigners. But Ms. V wanted us to see these things.

Back in town, we meet the head of an NGO that works on development issues. He is eager to talk about what his government does to hilltribes. "The question is not whether mistreatment and torture happen in this state," he says. "The question is how you guys can get the word out to stop these things."

He shows us his legs—a bruiselike scar across one shin and another scar running up the back of the opposite leg. "I have no tendons here," he says. "Courtesy of Big Brother…I've been in and out of prison." He was shackled, which caused him to lose muscle and acquire diseases that altered his skin and underlying tissue. "I was in solitary confinement," he says. "I've had a lot of bad experiences."

He leaves the room and soon returns with a photo album containing pictures of himself with Aung San Suu Kyi. "This is my home. She came to see me." It was in 1988. He points to another photo with the two of them among monks who helped organize the infamous uprising against the government that year. At least three thousand protesters were killed in the crackdown. The last photo he shows us depicts his "good friend," whom he hasn't seen since 1988. "They say that he died in the jungle, but I don't think so," he tells us. "He had an unfortunate accident."

In addition to his NGO, he runs a trekking service. He confirms that every area we visited is technically off-limits, illegal. "But all the guides will take you there, and the villagers will not say anything." After all, they earn money through tourism. "But I think you would have a problem if somebody saw you there."

This man tells us precisely what kind of place we have just seen. It's the kind of place where we can hike in bucolic wonder, gazing upon limestone cliffs, wandering amid patterned fields of sesame and ginger, gathering around household fires with villagers and their cats, chatting about plate tectonics while dining on curry and peanuts and fragrant bean salad. It's the kind of place where we can share happy moments with villagers.

But all the while, beneath that contented veneer, is a viral undercurrent of truth. And so people—like this man we meet in his shop—will tell us about the torture he endured, and he will show us pictures of the friend who disappeared. He will tell us about the poppies that people do in fact still grow in these hills, and warlords with lucrative pockets who rule in cahoots with "Big Brother."

The night approaches, and all the surrounding shops close. Our confidante smokes a cheroot by candlelight. He looks at Jerry and says, "So you're a freelance photographer." It's a statement, not a question. And Jerry explains—with knowing glances all around—that he's a construction worker, I'm a cook, but we're quite certain we were watched closely in Rangoon, and we wish to bring this man no harm.

"Yes, well I am the one who would be in hot water," he says. "You were careful in Yangon? You were careful who you talked to?" Some of the most unassuming people can be moles, he says.

We tell him we didn't talk to anyone.

He confirms everything, every rumor we have heard. He's had a rough life, but "I think Big Brother is giving up on me." He thinks, perhaps, they won't try to whisk him away, "again," for he has a lot of international support. He sees himself as hope incarnate. "I am the light at the end of the tunnel."

But he laments the lack of international government support. "Your country doesn't care about Burma." The United States can bomb Iraq, but Burma has not as much oil to offer, he says. The United States can send helicopters for drug enforcement programs, but the government uses those copters to bomb the people, he says. When foreigners offer BMW motorcycles as aid, they are used in motorcades, ushering generals through the country in style.

He talks of an American woman who promised him thousands of dollars for one of his projects, but the money never transpired. Americans, he says, want deadlines. They want to distribute money, tell people what to do, and get the job done promptly, efficiently. That isn't the way he works with villagers. "They don't learn anything by that." Instead he teaches as he builds walls. He makes buildings, but he also builds community by teaching people they can question authority, they can share ideas, they can stand up for what they think. He constructs the basis of democracy before he builds a wall. "Sometimes I purposely make mistakes," he says, just so he can apologize and the people can witness an authority figure saying sorry.

And he spotlights women. "Men do not have very good ideas," he says. Not when it comes to domestic questions. But women fetch the water, cook and clean and raise the kids. They have ideas on how these things could work better. But they are shocked when he asks their opinions—no one else does.

He's introducing child spacing, condoms, and women's health care. Here, as in many Asian societies, more kids are seen as better. They can care for younger siblings, tend the buffalo, and care for their aged parents as adults. These are difficult concepts to change, but he's trying. And sometimes the effort threatens his life.

Once, he says, a German journalist came and "I risked my butt" to help him meet several military porters who were horribly abused and disfigured. "We did not go together." The German took a guide from Kalaw. He came from one direction, the porters from another. "We did not meet here. We met in the hills." They talked, photos were taken, notes were scrawled. "He thought he had a scoop." But when the journalist returned to Germany the magazine editor told him the people are "not so interested in Burma at this time," and the story never ran.

Our informant tells us of another time while wandering through the mountains, when he became lost. He often visits villages in restricted areas, to reach people in need. But that time, he came upon a large military camp and the soldiers roughed him up. What are you doing? Where are you going? "Oh, I'm sorry, I'm sorry," he apologized. "I was wearing trousers and spoke to them in Burmese." They thought he was just a silly, confused Shan man and eventually let him go. He calls his country's own military "the occupational forces."

The military is, he says, everything we've heard it to be. "They can take any land they want for any reason." The people do not own their fields, thus they can never win economically. "Private ownership is the key to a strong economy," he says. But the military can relocate people on a whim. Some of the worst atrocities happen in Kayah State. "There are many internally displaced people." In the nineties, he says, the military blew up a large cross at the entrance to a Kayah town. Many Christians—the predominant religion there—were killed. "I have one girl, she saw them kill her father in front of her." He was a devout Christian and would never bow to another. But the soldiers took him at gunpoint while his young daughter watched. They told him to kneel before Buddha and he said OK, he will, but just don't shoot me in front of my daughter. They did anyway, between his eyes.

So he is helping the daughter, another of his projects.

He says soldiers "recruit" monks among the buffalo boys. The kids go to the fields, and soon they're destined for Rangoon monasteries. They're sometimes five or six years old, young enough to forget their native tongue and culture after significant time and indoctrination. And they never go home. Once, such a "recruitment" effort was witnessed by another boy. There was a fight, there were injuries, people found out, and there was outcry. But, like many stories, it has little chance of reaching outside ears.

He has dedicated his life to the cause of human rights and seems to think he has little to lose. "Maybe I'll have an unfortunate accident." That's how many stories end, he says. But until then, he fights.

Jerry takes his photo, and our confidante lights a cheroot. "Don't put me on the Internet," he says. Then he tells us, "I hope you can write something about this country."

When we leave, we tell him we hope to see him again, hope we can return. And he replies with chilling words.

"I hope I'm still alive then."

Right: A Pa-O man smokes a hand-rolled cheroot, the Burmese cigar, in his home in rural Shan State, Burma.

Following page: A teenage girl carries her young brother across the muddy street of Kyautsu, a small village in the Shan State, Burma. She wears thanaka paste on her cheeks to ward off sunburn and high-heeled wooden sandals to keep her feet out of the mud.

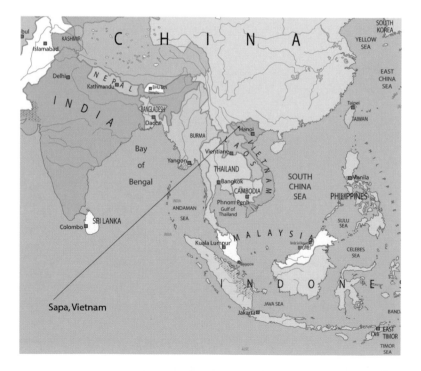

Sapa, Vietnam

17. Inbox - 2009

hello from shu
From: shusapa shusapa
Sent: Mon 4/13/09
Dear Karen and Jerry!
How are you?
i am shu from sapa. are you remember me?
few days ago I found me in the goole at your wedsite,
i am very happy, but iam not sure you boths still remember me or not,
i hope to hear from you soon
love shu

RE: hello from shu
From: Karen Coates & Jerry Redfern
Sent: 4/14/09
Shu,

I can't believe it's you—what a surprise to find your e-mail! Thank you for
writing. I have long wondered about you. How are you? How is your family?
I remember you very well; in fact, the story you found was something I wrote
after our encounter 10 years ago (I can't believe it's been that long). Many people
have read that story and said they loved it and learned a lot about Hmong life
because of it. I hope you don't mind. When I wrote it, we were living in a part
of the United States where most people knew nothing about Hmong culture or

what it is like to live in Vietnam.

I Googled your name and see that you now have a trekking group with the help of a few Australians, yes? That is great news! I'm so happy for you. I also found several travel blogs talking about your great guiding services. How is your business?

And how are your parents? I remember meeting them; please send them our best wishes.

Jerry and I are in Bangkok right now. We just arrived yesterday after spending 6 weeks in Cambodia. Much has happened in the last 10 years; we lived for a long time in Thailand, and Cambodia again. But in 2007, we bought a house in the United States and we now spend half the year in the US, the other half in Asia working.

We have not been back to Sapa since the time we met you, although we have traveled to Vietnam more recently. I would really like to visit you again—maybe late this year or early next year we can visit Sapa again. I would like to climb Fansipan!

It's so great to hear from you—please write again and tell us more about your life now.

Very best wishes,

Karen (and Jerry)

shu

From: shusapa shusapa

Sent: Wed 4/15/09 7:13 AM

Dear Karen and jerry!

i am very happy to hear from you boths,

i am fine and everything going ok,my family is well too, the bussines still not coming yet,but i have a job for be tour guide long time ago. around 6 years now,off coure no problem I am so happy that you made that story from me, and iam can not remember what is say , and remid a lot the thing for myself,

my english still not good, speaking is better, thank you so much contrac with me,

my life had been change a lot since we met, I hope that one day, we can sit down and talking about the story we had met before,

in here some picture from me and my daughter,i just want to tell you what iam look like now , not chagne much, now iam 22years old,

i hope to meet you soon,

please keep in touch

i miss you

love shu

RE: shu

From: Karen Coates & Jerry Redfern

Sent: 4/16/09

Shu,

Thank you so much for sending the pictures. Again, it's great to hear from you! You look just as you did before—I recognized your face immediately.

I've written about you and your e mail on my blog (I have a food blog, http:// ramblingspoon.com/blog) and posted a few small photos that I happened to have on my laptop.

I'm glad to hear you and your family are fine. And your daughter! How old is she? What is her name?

I really do hope we can return to Sapa next year. Please keep in touch!

Do you know, you are about the same age as my niece. It's so weird to think about that.

-Karen (and Jerry)

RE: shu

From: shusapa shusapa

Sent: 4/16/09

Dear Karen!

thank you so much for your email i am very happy to hear from you,

my daughter name is NGOC CHAU(pajdeg) and she is 3half years old,

i am still are busy to work, so now she already go to kids garden, so how are you boths?? do you have any children,

i am very happy that you both are remember me. yes i will be very happy to see you in here vietnam,

i will try to learn english better and write to you, every day i try to learn new word,

ok i hope to hear from you soon

shu

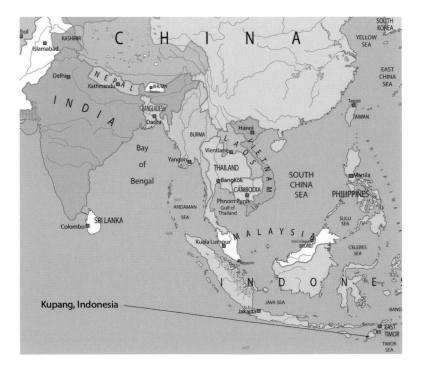

18. Sisters on the Sea - 2002

The sun sets in pink, purple, and Creamsicle streaks blazing through a film of clouds. One mountain, its edges nipped by the falling sun, rises higher than all the others, reaching for the floating sky. It is home to Semara, Balinese god of love.

For three days, the Indonesian ferry KM Awu sails away from Semara and toward Kupang. Three days, and endless hours gazing across open seas that surround a divided island. After centuries of colonization, decades of occupation, and years of warfare, Timor Island now splits between two nations. Kupang, in the west, belongs to Indonesia. The island's eastern half belongs to the newly independent and democratic nation of East Timor.

As I lean against the railing, watching the ocean spray, a woman named Dannie introduces herself. She works for the UN as well as a women's NGO in Kupang. She's five months into a six-month holiday, heading home after a long stretch in Bali. "I have to see my parents for a month," she says. She's traveling with her two-year-old son while her other son is with her Australian husband. He's working in Bangkok for a year—social work during the week, medical work on the weekends. He was deported from Indonesia, she says, when the authorities accused him of overstaying his visa. They called him a spy. Police rapped on their door and demanded he pay them 10 million rupiah ($1,070). They didn't have that kind of money, she says. "I hate the government," she fumes. "The government only hurts people."

Dannie tells me she is a mix of East and West, a woman of both Timors with relatives on both sides. Her people have moved across borders during tough times of fighting between the Indonesian military and the Timorese. She offers us a room in her mother's home, in a small village near the East/West line. That house has served as a refuge for friends in trouble.

But she says we'll be fine traveling overland to Dili, the East Timor capital. "I guarantee it." She visited the year before—when the city lay in ruins, destroyed in the fighting that led to independence.

Dannie tells me about her work, educating villagers about sanitation. "Timor is so bad," she says. "It's so bad." People "don't know how to clean themselves." So many years of upheaval have left catastrophes in health and social services. People don't understand germs and the path to disease, she says. Some women take contraceptives, "but they still have children." Too many children to feed.

Two months earlier, Jerry and I sat in a Cambodian hotel room watching East Timor's independence celebrations—a brand new country in the twenty-first century. "We should go there," we agreed. Now here we are, floating along, thinking of what lies ahead.

*****

I'm sitting in a dank cave of a room with fourteen young, sober Indonesian men in pants, listening to a fledgling band screeching cheesy renditions of 1970s easy listening Top 40 tunes. The stage glows in a flood of red light, and the room shakes with painful, leaden Casio keyboard vibrations. The men's pants, apparently, are important—a bouncer at the door checks that every man wears them. Jerry returns to the room to change from shorts, which are as unwelcome as sandals with bare toes. I've covered my feet in bright white running socks beneath my Tevas for the pleasure of witnessing this.

Out on deck on a passageway bulkhead is a diagram of this ship with a little pictogram of a martini glass with an olive, the universal code for alcohol. That's why we're here. Yet there is no bar at the bar. There is no alcohol on this ship adrift among seventeen thousand islands of mostly Muslim tendencies. So we have a ship at sea, we have a so-called bar, we have an audience in pants, we have a stage with red lights, we have an unpalatable band and nothing to smooth the edges.

Now a woman takes the stage, singing beneath alternating flashing spotlights. She's dressed in a skimpy tight spaghetti-strap black little thing, though she herself is no little thing.

She bellows something deep and throaty in an earthy voice.

Wait…I can hear it.

It's Neil Diamond.

The singer invites a young man in a yellow windbreaker to dance with her on-stage. He sways his shoulders side to side while twirling in circles, as though his sense of balance were suddenly switched off. She shakes her booty.

The room bloats with men, more and more filing through the non-bar's doors. No drinking, no smoking, no slurring. Yet the majority seems to enjoy this. That is, except for one obviously unhappy young man in the way back. He rolls his eyes and shakes his head. As the singers croon, he sighs with visible distaste and hollers a request: "Please! For Bon Jovi!"

*****

Amid the din, I meet a woman named Florence. "I think you have work in East Timor," she shouts over the noise. Since no tourists go to Timor anymore, she guesses I must be on my way to business. Florence studies law in Bali. She is young and pretty and vivacious, with long dark hair pushed high on her head and tumbling down her shoulders. She's East Timorese. She's on school break, and she's heading home to visit family in both Atambua, the last town on the Indonesian side of the border; and Dili, the new Timorese capital. Her father is a police officer, a very heavy personality in Atambua. "If you have problem, you can call my father." She repeatedly offers this service and tells me about two of her friends who were recently caught with drugs, a crime punishable by death in Indonesia. So when the police picked up her friends, Florence called her father and her friends were let go with a simple warning: "Next time, please don't bring that."

This is what she tells me, but it's hard to decipher all that she's saying over the ruckus on stage. She tells us repeatedly it's no problem for us to go to Dili, to cross the border. "It's OK now." Yet she later alludes to problems I don't fully understand. Much is lost in translation. Perhaps she's saying more than she's saying. Or maybe she's lived so long in conflict that her barometer for trouble is calibrated differently. One woman's danger is another woman's normal.

Florence says she was in Atambua in 1999 and she saw three foreigners killed that year because they worked in East Timor and the Indonesian government didn't like it. "Yes, I saw. It was very bad." I have not heard of that incident, but I am well aware of the widely publicized case in 2000, in which pro-Indonesian militias in Atambua killed three UN workers, beating them and burning their bodies. It's now almost two years later—perhaps painful memories are fading.

Florence leaves us with one important instruction. "You are tourists," she says. "When they ask you questions, say you are tourists at the border."

*****

For three days, the world around us exists in varying shades of blue. Water draws a tight line against the sky. The blue above stands still while the blue below rocks like a cradle. But the line never changes—always straight, constant. Just a few cargo ships to break its stubborn way.

People scatter across the decks, lounging on black padded cushions, in corners, along walkways, with all manner of boxes and fruits and clothes and suitcases. There's a stash of bikes on deck. One passenger travels with a new, plastic-wrapped double mattress.

There are brown feet on wooden benches, people napping in the sun, people squatting against the railing, people lingering around the cafeteria stairwell, people shuffling rubber sandals around and around the deck, people piled on mats in every conceivable space, people smoking, people yakking, people hawking piles of CDs and pens and other stuff. There are people everywhere, which, after all, is a key Indonesian attribute—the impressive sum of its people. And for the great sums that the West doesn't know of this country—the largest country with a Muslim majority and the world's fourth most populous—it should know at least that: the sum of its people, so close to 250 million.

We are at the moment ourselves an Indonesian island let loose, moving in knots. We've turned so the sun catches my legs from the side, no longer dead-on, and I see another mountain sprouting from the sea on another island along our trail—the trail of Indonesia itself. The country is a spray of volcanoes and lava and reefs and sand tossed across the waters of the Southern Hemisphere. Water defines the very nature of this country, a string of diversity joined by this steadfast horizon on a cobalt canvas. That horizon and the waters beneath the southern night sky are arguably the only things this nation truly shares. Even the daytime sky shifts from place to place, dumping storms over one island while baking others. But the horizon and its platter of water wrap from one end to the other, linking all.

*****

We stop at Waingapu, where a sea of humanity descends upon the docks and another wave washes over the ship. Thousands show up for the spectacle, sending away loved ones, picking up friends, retrieving sacks, moving chests, knitting a blanket of human movement. Like ants, people file off the ship on one ramp while others embark on another. A Polisi officer with a megaphone keeps order, shooing the crowd as people and their assorted cargo come off. There's a chest of drawers, that plastic-wrapped mattress, a 6- by 3-foot picture frame with nothing inside. A sack of Thai sugar, a box of Indonesian salt, a kid's bike in bubble wrapping, two color TVs, two stereo speakers, many boxes marked "Abba Ministries," and another box destined for someone named Nathalia.

The dock workers wear orange. They're all young men with unruly long hair and sweat cascading down their faces. One accidentally kicks a green vase into the wall. It breaks, and the young man is deeply chagrined. He hits his head in shame.

"Buka, buka, buka!" the officer shouts. He wants the crowd to part so passengers can make their way through. And so goes the tide for two more hours until we return to sea.

*****

At 2:30 a.m. the ship stops in Ende, but I stay in bed. A young woman in the upper bunk turns on the lights and packs her goods, moving boxes to the front door. Then a young man enters the room and helps with her luggage. She creeps out the door in silence. I have heard this woman say nothing the entire trip.

This ship is segregated by gender, and I'm sharing a four-bunk cabin with women who sleep an extraordinary amount. I come and go, but I always return to a room with lights on and eyes closed. My cabinmates rise for meals, then scuttle back to their den of rest, and I see them nowhere else on the boat. They do not speak English, but the woman in bunk C smiles kindly and one day she brushes my shoulder when we pass each other in the dining room.

All I can imagine—for I really know nothing of their lives—is that these women are here on this boat on a solitary sea away from husbands and children who otherwise require constant attention and time. But here on this ship, they have no obligations but their own comfort of mind. So we cruise through the world, and they sleep.

But things change at 5 a.m. The door opens and a man and woman enter, surprised to find me sleeping. They're siblings, and the man asks me to talk with his sister to keep her company. But then he does all the talking—go figure. The man, named Jack, doesn't seem to understand this is a women-only room. He likes to chat. He tells me, apropos of nothing, that he studied at technical school and works with his sister's husband on Flores Island, building bridges and roads. They live in Kupang but have work on Flores. He gives me his address and offers to show me around Kupang. He asks what I studied in school, and I tell him writing. He turns to his sister and motions with his hands as though he's revving a motorcycle. Riding. He asks if I've gone to university. I tell him yes. I studied writing. Writing and anthropology. I still don't know if he understands.

When our two other roommates arrive, Jack leaves and the Indonesian women start up a conversational storm. Silence flees in an instant. The cabin fills with the rolled Rs, deep-throated syllables, and open vowels of Indonesian diction. I wish I could understand all the world's languages for precisely these moments in rooms among other women on a journey, so I could understand what in the world is on their minds and out their mouths. This happens everywhere, but especially among strangers such as these who meet for the first time on a mutual expedition.

A passenger watches Bali disappear astern at sunset from aboard the Pelni passenger and cargo ship Awu.

They share a language, and they share a bond simply by being female. I've seen this happen in Indonesia and Vietnam; in Japan, Laos, Cambodia, China, Tibet, and Thailand. But I'm not sure I've seen it at home, not among strangers so quickly, naturally, fluidly.

It's as though Asian women share a gene that overrides boundaries of class and family and prescribed social divisions; as though all women are, by nature, what their languages call them:

Sisters.

Dili, East Timor

19. Dr. Dan - 2002

It's Saturday and the door is closed. He's inside. Outside: babies cry, mothers pace, children sniffle, and fathers sit still with arms crossed. There's a row of seats along a yellow wall where thousands of people have sat sweating and waiting, waiting and sweating over the years. All of those people, leaning against that yellow wall, have left shadowy marks of heads and backs above each chair. One small blue sign hangs above the door with crisp white letters. It says plain and simple: DR. DAN.

His patients come by the hundreds, every day, in the beds of dusty pickup trucks or in taxis that cost a week's pay. They wear their Sunday best. They make it a special event. They wait and wait, outside that door, clinging to the strings of a delicate hope: perhaps the American doctor will cure them.

Dr. Daniel Murphy has worked in East Timor since 1998, when it was still part of Indonesia. He worked with Indonesian tanks razing the streets, helicopters swooping over his roof, gunshots shattering human bone. He worked while houses burned and bodies were dumped in the sea. The Indonesians deported him, they blacklisted him, but he made his way back. "Security is not even an issue," he says. "You can't think about it. You just gotta do what you gotta do."

What Dr. Dan says he's gotta do is help people until there is no more need.

Jerry and I have come to follow the story of this American physician, a legend in this new country, recently reborn and newly independent. On May 20, 2002, East Timor took its own reins. It became the world's newest nation, and for the first time in recorded history, it faced a future alone. For 450 years, Portugal colonized the eastern half of Timor Island, a remote outpost cast between Indonesia and Australia. That ended with a coup in Lisbon in 1974. Indonesian soldiers invaded the year after, and they stayed twenty-four more. Since then, documents and transcripts and witnesses have surfaced to substantiate this brutal indictment: the day before the invasion, U.S. President Ford's administration told Indonesia it was OK to invade.

The Indonesians entered with a mission of "encirclement and annihilation." They maimed, tortured, mutilated, burned. One-fourth of the Timorese population was killed in the Indonesian occupation. The people eventually voted for independence in a 1999 referendum, which they won after a heinous fight. The United Nations intervened and, now, a new nation is rising in the ashes of two hundred thousand dead.

*****

Dr. Dan was there through the country's worst times, and he has every intention to stay. He comes from Iowa. He spent six years with César Chávez and his farmers. He's worked in Laos, Nicaragua, and Mozambique. Here, his Bairo Pité Clinic prescribes free hope to a people conditioned by dismay.

Dr. Dan wears a salt-and-pepper beard and running shoes on active feet. He sees patients six days a week. On Sundays and lunch breaks, he oversees a tuberculosis clinic. On vacations abroad, he raises money and speaks about East Timor's plight. He never rests—he did, once, while suffering a bout of falciparum malaria, the deadliest kind. For that, he took one afternoon off in the solitude of East Timor's inland mountains.

Dr. Dan's principles allow no room for vacations. East Timor is among the world's poorest countries. It has no medical school, no specialists, few native doctors, and few diagnostic tools. Tuberculosis, malaria, gastroenteritis, and pneumonia run rampant. Women die in childbirth and children die young. "Our health care system is overwhelmed with things that wouldn't have to be here," Murphy says.

The year 1999 eclipses all others. Fighting after the August referendum led to a "total collapse of the East Timor health system," according to the United Nations. Seventy-five percent of the people fled their homes, and more than 80 percent of those homes were burned to the ground. Health centers were razed. Only twenty-five doctors remained in the country; others fled to Indonesia.

Now, half the country falls below the poverty line, while the under- and unemployment rates top 70 percent. Malaria is highly endemic, and half of all kids are undernourished. Infant and under-5 mortality rates are among the region's highest, and the country has but one physician for every ten thousand people.

*****

Jerry and I squeeze through Dr. Dan's door as one patient leaves and another one enters. He welcomes us warmly but warns us he can only talk between exams. So I sit against the wall and Jerry stands on the side with cameras in hand. We watch just a smidgen of the life that defines Dr. Dan.

"One Monday we had 650," he says. "I challenge anyone to sit down and see that many patients." He's examined hundreds of thousands in all, and the number swells every day. In and out, in and out, in a minute or two. No one knocks; they just enter. He sees them all, swiveling his chair, scrawling prescriptions, talking to me, living out a doctrine of grassroots health care. His critics say he works too fast, diagnosing without digging deep enough. But he counters that he does all he can to help the greatest number. It's the only way, he says.

Dr. Dan talks about the election in 1999, when 98.6 percent of voters went to the polls and 78 percent chose freedom. That didn't sit well with Indonesia or its militia supporters. "Everyone was thrown out of the country." He was, too. He had worked at another clinic in Dili, but when he returned, he found a city in flames. He found this vacant house and started anew. "This building was one of the few that wasn't on fire." He treated any and all, ignoring the guns and tanks as best he could.

There were others like Dr. Dan at the time, professionals who risked their lives to save the dying. A young nurse at the Bairo Pité Clinic who calls himself Jhony worked in the Dili hospital then. Women were raped, men shot and stabbed, children torn to pieces. "Lots of people died in front of me," he says. Supplies were slim; they reused needles because they had no choice. Jhony says he helped all patients, Timorese or Indonesian, because that's what he was trained to do. But the Indonesians and their militiamen threatened him for helping their enemies. They told him, "Why do you want to help the Timorese? They're nothing.

They're stupid."

East Timor grabbed world attention then, with Dili burning and people dying. In those days, Dr. Dan did interviews all the time—like this, between the swing of patients through his door. He had to tell East Timor's story while he had a global audience, he says. It was a story unlike any other.

"I've never seen a situation where a whole population did absolutely nothing to bring this down on themselves," he says.

"It just came."

*****

The door opens.

Dr. Dan turns to examine a little boy, diarrhea, four days in a row. "I just worry about giardia." Then he tends to the mother, who delivered a child at home and has a sore that won't heal. "Complications of pregnancy are very common here. Women die in childbirth all the time."

Dr. Dan works on a shoestring budget and a heavy tweed of love. He can't cure more than the basics; he hasn't time to investigate the mysterious. Cancer, heart disease, AIDS: there is little hope in this country. There is no chemotherapy, no bypass surgery, no complicated drug cocktails. First-world health is beyond what he can offer.

The door.

A woman with epilepsy enters. She reacted badly to the first drug he prescribed, and Dr. Dan can't find enough of an alternative. He combs the world in order to fill rare prescriptions. When foreigners tell Dr. Dan they're coming to visit, he asks them to bring stashes of medicines. "I always have a list ready," he says.

The door.

Two men assist an older woman with scars across her left breast. It's probably cancer. She went to a traditional healer who meant well but left her marred. She's beyond surgery; even if she weren't, there are no surgeons in East Timor to perform it. "So this doesn't look good," Dr. Dan says. "Two months of lumps and now pain in the bones. But there's hope." He has a medicine that sometimes helps cancer patients.

He doesn't tell the woman she will probably die. He tells her he has some pills, he can't guarantee they will work, but he will try. He says the woman knows her prognosis; her village neighbors have told her it's cancer. She, like most Timorese in Dr. Dan's experience, took the news in stride. After so much brutality, the people have mentally reconciled their fate, he says. They accept death as a cycle of life. They must, to stay sane. "You have to come up with some pretty good mechanisms for that—and one of them would be not to think of the future at all."

Most of Dr. Dan's patients are women, and he has a simple explanation for that: "Men have almost all been killed. Half of the population is aged fifteen and below. So this is basically a country of women and children."

He talks of an eighteen-year-old girl with a congenital heart defect. In Australia or Europe or America, she'd be fine. In East Timor, she will die. So Dr. Dan goes to work online, soliciting donors, seeking visas, searching for connections.

Money is always a problem. The government pays some staff salaries. The state pharmacy offers basic medicines. But that leaves a gap of thousands for him to cover each month, to sustain a few dozen workers, a tuberculosis wing, a lab, a laundry, a kitchen, a maternity ward, and trips to the mountains for outbound care. He scrimps and scrapes to pay the bills. The power fails, the patients are hungry. "We used to get rice from an NGO. Now we don't." When the violence stopped, people quit donating, as though East Timor's ills were cured by peace. "The work is really just beginning."

The door.

A man enters. "He just had a little abscess on his head," Dr. Dan says. "He was beaten up by the militia in '99 and it flares up every so often."

Murphy struggles to stay focused through a day of so many patients. "I have to think about every second, every word, every motion." But he feels personally compelled to talk about why he is here. He knows his country's role in East Timor's past. "So when I think I'm working, and my taxes are going to do this, I feel guilty…how can we even dare raise our heads anywhere after doing this?" He thinks of the mountain folk who came down from the hills to vote for freedom. He thinks about their fear of being killed. He thinks of how many times that fear proved right. "The world shouldn't be like this. Something has to change."

He goes on and on. He does this from time to time, as patients silently wait. And I feel acutely conscious of moments slipping away, precious time pilfered from people in need. Then he gains control, refocuses, and apologizes for the digression. "Sorry for getting emotional," he says.

The door.

A woman enters and Dr. Dan pecks her on the cheek. "She had a baby during the worst crisis time." No hospital. No doctors. The baby was born with no anus. The only surgeon available worked for the Indonesian Army. Dr. Dan personally asked him to help with this Timorese woman's child—an enemy by politics but an obligation by professional creed. The surgeon operated, and the child survived.

The door.

A patient he'd seen before. "This woman was very sick last week. Near death." Stricken with typhoid, burning up, but better now. "When I see people like her get better it makes me feel like at least we're doing something."

He tells the story of a woman in labor, whom he helped the year before. She had trouble with delivery. The placenta wouldn't come out. She lived just a few blocks from the clinic, but she didn't go. Instead, Dr. Dan went to her. He found her on the dirt floor. She had been too embarrassed to go to the clinic because she didn't have clothes for the baby.

*****

The afternoon goes on, the patients in and out. "It's just a constant stream. All day." Dr. Dan says he's used to it. It was worse when he first came to East Timor. "No air conditioning. I had that wooden chair," he says, pointing to a patient's chair, "and can you imagine trying to see five hundred to six hundred people? And that's with tanks, helicopters…" His voice trails off. Now he has an adjustable swivel chair, a present from an Australian. It's a small gift, but a cherished one that eases the doctor through wearying days.

*****

The sun starts to fade through the windows, but Dr. Daniel Murphy is not finished, not even close, perhaps never. "My work is done when everybody's healthy. So far that hasn't happened."

 The doctor stays until the last patient leaves, around dark. Then he heads to his computer, alone, in a quiet, secluded room. He connects to his network of friends and colleagues around the world, seeking donations and dispensing information on East Timor.

The stream of Bairo Pité patients ceases with the sun because they're not used to going out at night. Darkness harbors fear and death, for those are the hours in which husbands, fathers, and brothers disappeared; the hours when sisters and wives were raped. But the patients will return again, on Monday morning, rising with the light. They will arrive before Dr. Dan does. They will fill every door, every bench, every seat, stoop, and sidewalk. And they will wait as long as it takes.

In the lab, technicians will probe for malaria and tuberculosis and parasites of the gut. They will peer through a microscope at tiny strips of glass. They will labor beneath a sign on the wall that says:

"Near Enough is Not Good Enough."

And it never is with Dr. Dan.

NOTE: This story first appeared in Drexel Online Journal in 2004. Since then, the country's health situation has improved somewhat, but East Timor still ranks among the region's lowest in health, economic, and development indicators. Dr. Dan's Bairo Pité Clinic welcomes volunteers and donations. For more information, see http://bairopiteclinic.org/.

19 - Dr. Dan - 2002

Dr. Dan Murphy fills out paperwork from his desk at the Bairo Pite Clinic.

19 - Dr. Dan - 2002

Patients line up and wait to see Dr. Dan Murphy at the Bairo Pite Clinic. His name is above the door.

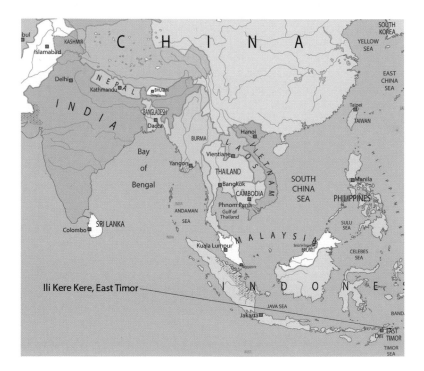

Ili Kere Kere, East Timor

20. Timor's Caves of Liberation - 2002

You can't just go to the cave; it requires a bit of ceremony. The appropriate men gather in a thatch pavilion, each one clutching a machete, chewing betel nut, smoking, and chattering with the man beside him. They sit on pink plastic chairs and wooden benches while a venerable gray-haired custodian assesses the situation. His name is Rafael Guimarez, and he decides yes or no. His cousin, Paolo da Costa, also decides yes or no. And their cousin, Enrique do Santos, also decides yes or no. If, and only if, all three agree, you may go to the cave.

After all, Ili Kere Kere Cave has helped shape the nation's history. It sits high on the side of a cliff at the eastern edge of Timor Island, a patch of land now split between Indonesia and East Timor. Archaeologists know that early humans passed through this landscape at least thirty thousand years ago. Tens of thousands of years later, they painted cave walls with fantastic designs. Pleistocene fishermen and Neolithic gardeners sheltered in these caves. And in much more recent years, guerrilla soldiers hid here from the marauding Indonesian Army.

Caves are central to Timorese identity, inherent in mythology and ritual. One legend tells of a long-ago flood that killed everyone but one man and one woman. The woman lived high on the limestone terraces of a cave; the man lived far below. She lowered a rope to her lover so he could meet her for conjugal visits. They had seven sons and seven daughters, from whom all of East Timor's people purportedly sprang.

*****

Jerry and I trek to the eastern tip of this new nation just a few months after East Timor celebrates independence from decades of brutal Indonesian occupation, following centuries of Portuguese colonization. We have heard about this region's magnificent seas, coral reefs, and fishermen with outrigger canoes who stay in caves on the beach. We read in a guidebook that somewhere in the nearby jungle is a cave with old paintings—but it's hard to find. And that is why we are here, in Tutuala village, surrounded by thirty men, with Rafael Guimarez deciding our fate.

Rafael is an old gentleman with burly feet, a betel-stained mouth, gray frizz on his head, and a lifetime of grit beneath his nails. He belongs to a family of cousins who have inherited responsibility for the upkeep of Ili Kere Kere, which sits on old family land. The three cousins guard the property through consensus. Paolo da Costa has given his OK. Enrique do Santos has gone to his garden for the day, and so we await Rafael's verdict. We offer him a cigarette, and he puffs.

In my notebook, I hastily craft three sentences in Tetum, one of East Timor's two official languages (the other being Portuguese): Ami journalistu America. Ami hakarak ba fatuk-kuak ba haree tinta, porfavor. Ami mai ba husa licensa. A sketchy attempt at: "We are American journalists. We would like to go to the cave to see the paintings, please. We come to ask permission."

All for naught, because we learn Guimarez doesn't speak Tetum—he speaks Fatuluku, one of the sixteen local languages spoken in this nation of eight hundred thousand people. Nonlocal languages include Portuguese, Bahasa Indonesia, and—rarely—English. So a man sitting nearby, twenty-nine-year-old Rozerio do Santos, translates, and words are exchanged in Fatuluku. Many words. Big words, small words, loud words, quiet words—and we have no idea what transpires. But somewhere amid all this chatter, Rafael apparently says it's fine for us to visit the cave, and it's fine for Jerry to take photos. Rozerio translates: We must pay ten dollars, the standard fee. Since Rozerio speaks English, he will guide us.

And off we go.

*****

Independence from Indonesia not only opened East Timor's door to democracy. It raised a window to science. Just months after the Timorese voted for independence in a 1999 referendum, a team of Australian archaeologists arrived to study the island's caves. They picked up where colleagues had left off decades earlier.

Before them, Ian Glover was the last scientist to excavate in the area, while he was a PhD student at Australian National University in the 1960s. He investigated Timor as a possible route for Pleistocene migration to Australia.

When Matthew Spriggs and Susan O'Connor of the ANU teamed up with Peter Veth of James Cook University in 2000 for the East Timor Archaeological Project, "there was no administration," Spriggs recalls. "We just hired a vehicle and drove around." They met Paolo da Costa in Tutuala and asked permission to study a cave called Lene Hara. "He said we were the first people that ever asked him."

On their second trip that year, the archaeologists excavated and found evidence of two possible phases of human occupation: as a transit camp between the coast and inland resources 30,000 to 35,000 years ago, then again as a possible shelter for Neolithic gardeners as far back as 12,000 years.

This is common for Timorese, keeping temporary shelters in huts and caves in addition to their full-time homes. Caves make good storage spots for grain, tobacco, and beans. They serve as corrals for goats and water buffalo, and they're sources of clean water. Even today, on weekends, villagers camp in rock shelters on the beaches below Ili Kere Kere, while they spearfish the abundant coral reef just offshore and cater to an influx of foreign aid workers on weekend break. Come Sunday afternoon, they huff back uphill to the village with a few extra dollars in their pockets from the fish they caught and grilled for expat visitors.

*****

When Spriggs returned to East Timor for the third time, villagers in the seaside town of Com told him they were proud to have helped Xanana Gusmao during his years as a guerrilla soldier fighting the Indonesians. Gusmao, who became East Timor's first president, is something of a legend. He had lived in a nearby cave—would Spriggs like to look? "No outsiders had ever seen it," Spriggs says.

The villagers showed him Uluana, a site with two caves. Gusmao's troops camped in one, and their leader in another three hundred feet uphill. If the Indonesians attacked, the guerrillas could give Gusmao time to escape. But the

Indonesians never found that camp. The fighters covered every trace. "You'd never know because there's nothing at all in these sites," Spriggs says. He's fascinated by that fact. "If you're an archaeologist, straight away you'd think that was kind of suspicious." Caves always have signs of previous life. But every day, the rebels meticulously cleaned their hovel.

Spriggs inspected a nearby watering hole, where the Indonesians had planned an ambush. But the Timorese never showed up. There, he found ration tins littering the streambed and the names of regiments of Indonesian soldiers scrawled on a tree—a stark contrast to Uluana. Another time, Spriggs excavated a place called Tele Punu, where families from the village of Com had taken refuge between 1975 and 1977. He traveled with Edmondo, the village head, who had spent his early years there. They had to bushwhack their way; no one had returned in more than twenty years. When Edmondo saw the site, memories flooded him. "He told me his mother had died of malaria in the cave because they had no medicine," Spriggs says. "He kept pulling out all these objects." He found an old bottle they had used as a lamp. He found a sharpening stone he recognized as his mother's. He found his bed.

*****

Rozerio leads Jerry and me down a steep gravel road from Tutuala. We pass little girls toting water and laundry and bathing paraphernalia in big baskets atop their heads. The village watering hole sits a mile and a half downhill. Every bath, every drink, every pot of soup requires a hike.

The crackled fields around us breathe a prayer for rain. Do Santos says another village once stood here, but a pro-Indonesian militia destroyed each home in 1983. He nods toward a tilting skeleton of a thatch home with a grave in front. The marker notes his brother's name: "Ernesto Pereira da Costa Lima. Sept. 23, 1951–May 28, 1997." The Indonesian Army captured Ernesto in 1997, accusing him of helping a younger brother, a Timorese rebel fighter. Ernesto told the Indonesians it wasn't true. "They said, 'You lie,' and they shoot him," Rozerio tells us.

On Sundays, Rozerio puts flowers on his brother's grave. He now lives with his brother's wife and supports the family. His other brother, the rebel, was caught in 1999 and vanished, as thousands of other Timorese did. "I don't know exactly where he is now." Rozerio also faced danger. "The army found me and wanted to kill me." So he fled to the surrounding hills, limestone cliffs in a jagged terrain that kept the Indonesians at bay—that time.

Farther along our walk, we pause at a concrete table on a beautiful overlook, and Rozerio says it was worth it—his brother's death, all the violence. Worth it, because this spot is safe. All the spots are safe. His people have independence. They are free to visit their own gardens now.

*****

From there, Rozerio takes us to a modest little house, where Paolo da Costa greets us in his yard and invites us inside. We sit in plastic chairs and he tells us his grandfather lived in Ili Kere Kere as a hermit. He and his cousins still pay regular homage with a pig, some eggs, and rice as gifts to the ancestors.

Da Costa sports a long gray beard and weathered skin. He says he remembers the Japanese occupation happened when he was not yet old enough to walk. That would have made him a toddler in 1942—and much younger than the seventy-five to eighty he thinks he is when we meet him. As with many villagers we find across Asia, young is young, old is old, history is memory, and the specifics don't matter so much as people's perceptions of those memories. It's one reason why hard science can be so frustrating around here.

But da Costa's eyes shimmer when he says he is proud his cave has acquired such elevated scientific status. "The archaeologists made a paper about the caves." He quickly disappears into his room, leaving us alone. I take inventory of his walls: an election poster of Gusmao, photocopied instructions for voting, and several pictures of Jesus. The 2002 national election results are scratched on notebook paper, showing Gusmao's 20,895 votes against his opponent's 1,212.

Da Costa returns. He gingerly displays, with outstretched arms, "Excavation at Lene Hara Cave," the O'Connor, Spriggs, Veth report. The crisp, white photocopies are "only to see, not to take," Rozerio explains seriously.

*****

Rozerio leads us a few kilometers to a dirt road that ends in a parking lot. From there, a raised concrete-slab walkway constructed in Indonesian times marks the way to Ili Kere Kere. He doesn't like the walkway. The Indonesians forced locals to build it, he says. "They have the power. If I don't do something, they shoot me."

We descend steep stairs to a rocky ledge with sweeping views of the sea. Then we spot the first figures: four men wielding tools above their heads, painted in red on the rock wall. We skirt a narrow path to the front, facing the water. The ground beneath our feet is slick with ages of human wear.

Pictures surround us, high and low, abstract and literal, in red, black, and yellow. A hand stencil, concentric circles, others with spokes and spikes, a spade with crescents. East Timor's caves are galleries of ancient art. Some catch the daylight, high on rocky terraces. Others linger in darkness, deep within tunnels. There are dancing red humans, hunters with spears, hand stencils, lizards, men on horseback, elaborate canoes, and a pair of tortoises devouring a fish. There are geometric designs in red, black, yellow, and green. They come in radiating suns, circles with spokes, heart shapes, and spiral labyrinths. The earliest paintings, archaeologists speculate, are somewhere between two thousand and four thousand years old.

Do Santos walks from picture to picture, dismayed. "Indonesians scratched," he says. "Formerly, there were many cave paintings," but only a fraction remain. He guides us around boulders and bends, to images of people, boats, and horses. "And here, the man fights a cock," he points out. "But it's not very clear." Many images are faint, almost impossible to distinguish. "It was very clear before the Indonesian army came here and destroyed."

Giant honeycombs dangle from a high rock overhang. "The honey is security," Rozerio says. It has fed generations of Timorese. Today, villagers still climb rickety scaffolding to reach that sweetness near the ceiling.

The afternoon dims, and it's time to go. As we head uphill and through the forest, we talk about East Timor's future. "I think for the people it is good; now East Timor has freedom," Rozerio says. "But the economy—it is a concern for everyone."

He does not regret the losses, the sacrifices people have made. "They say that the victims are every family, but not in vain. We have independence. We died, but not in vain."

He asks whether we think another colonizer will come to East Timor. The question surprises us, and we tell him we don't think so. But he disagrees. "I think maybe."

*****

Within a few months of our visit, riots erupt in the capital, Dili. Militiamen with homemade knives and AK-47s kill at least four villagers in the far west of the country. They say they are armed by Kopassus, the Indonesian special forces, with orders to kill Timorese leaders. Fear returns to the countryside.

But on that warm fall day with Rozerio, we head back to Paolo da Costa's house in a peaceful mood. He offers arak, a strong homemade whiskey. We slug it back and smack our lips.

Paolo says he would like his photo taken, a formal picture. He disappears again into the bedroom and emerges in a beautiful tais cloth of black, red, green, and white threads, which his wife made by hand.

He wears a bright yellow and pink sash, and traditional beads handed down through the generations. In the center of his chest is a large brass medallion, the size of a CD.

Paolo da Costa stands barefoot on the rocky earth, displaying the ancient garb of his people as a newly free man.

Right: A spear fisherman holds up his catch from the waters near Tutuala, East Timor.

Below: Rozerio do Santos holds his hand up to a painted hand design that has been ruined in recent years. He claims that Indonesian troops defaced the ancient paintings of Ili Kere Kere Cave, on the far eastern tip of East Timor. Archaeologists do not know what all of the cave's painted designs mean. The paintings, they speculate, date somewhere between 2,000 and 4,000 years old. Archaeologists believe that people first occupied East Timor's caves about 30,000 years ago. They also think that Timor may have been a route for early humans migrating to Australia.

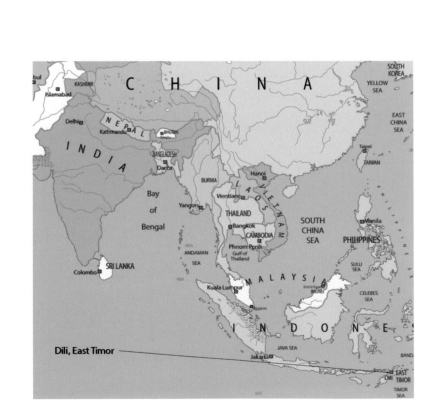

Dili, East Timor

21. DiliDiliDiliDiliDiliDili - 2002

There is only one bus from Los Palos to Dili. At ten minutes before 3 a.m., the engine starts. At precisely three, the shouting begins: DiliDiliDiliDiliDiliDili-Dili! DiliDiliDiliDiliDiliDili! DiliDiliDili! DiliDiliDili!

Headlights shine through our window in a shabby hotel in tiny Los Palos on the eastern edge of East Timor. We arrived from Dili just the afternoon before, so this is certainly not our bus. Dilidilidilidilidilidili! a young man hollers until slowly the headlights fade, taking the yelling with them, and I think, OK, they're gone. I can sleep again. But half an hour later, it's back. Dilidilidilidilidilidili-lidilidili!

Apparently the bus doesn't go directly to Dili: it drives around. Around and around and around. Around the darkened streets, casting the only light on a sleeping Los Palos. And noise. It casts a lot of noise.

That bus turns down every street in town once, twice, three times, more, calling for passengers to Dili, until finally, with the town's coterie of roosters in full crow, the driver makes a right turn instead of a left, and sets sail for the capital some 110 miles west.

Of course, one morning, after a week of tromping about the eastern cape of the country, our time comes and we need to catch the bus to Dili. We try to communicate with the people who run the guesthouse, and they tell us that the bus leaves in the morning. Maybe at six. Remembering the cacophony from our previous stay in town, we don't rise before three. Yet by 4:50 Jerry and I are dressed and packed; we've washed, we've peed. Sleep was impossible. We carefully exit through the hotel's screechy gate and we wait at the street. There is the bus in the distance: Dilidilidilidilidilidili. Faint but familiar. Growing closer. DiliDiliDILIDILI.

It rounds the corner and stops. We get on. There is no one on board aside from the driver, the yeller, and one young man sitting alone. We take our seats and listen to the yeller, a young guy with a flap of curly hair beneath a tightly tied bandana, yodeling Dilidilidilidili to all the deserted streets.

The driver turns, again, onto the main street, right in front of our hotel, away from Dili.

"What time does the bus leave?" Jerry asks.

And he, this teenager who screeches from the bottom of his larynx to the tip of his tongue for hours, utters such a faint and feeble mew we can barely decipher the words.

"Six," he whispers.

So on the next loop through town we get off and sit on the hotel stoop and watch the stars and listen to the crickets as the bus continues its circuit.

At 5:35 we hear the bus again and the young man's voice draws closer. We get on, and the original passenger boards again just up the road (apparently he got off, too). This time, a family sits in the back of the otherwise empty bus. It's just that family, the original passenger, the driver, screamer boy, and us.

DiliDiliDiliDiliDiliDiliDILIDILIDILI!

"We will go around two more times," the original passenger tells us with a hint of desperation because, he says, this ride for him is "urgent." He has a flight to catch in Dili. "We should be there by twelve," he says.

"Why does this happen?" we ask. Why this bus going round and round; why this incessant yelling?

"The bus has to find people," he answers.

Why not have a schedule? Why not tell people the bus leaves at six?

"But maybe the people don't know the bus leaves at six," he says. "Maybe someone has to go now." Not that we're really going anywhere.

DiliDiliDiliDiliDiliDILIDILIDILI!

So round and round we go, every now and then picking up a straggler or two. Then, precisely at six, just when I think we'll turn left as we have so many times before, we turn right instead.

And we head to Dili.

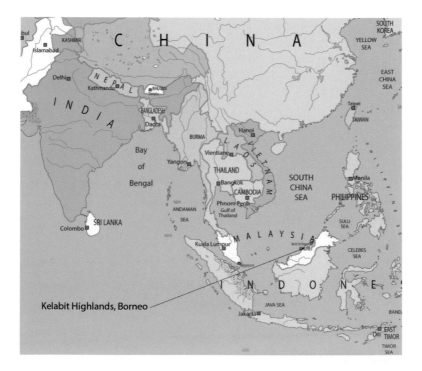

Kelabit Highlands, Borneo

22. And We Eat Pig - 2006

"Do you want to see hunting?" Sylvester asks.

We sit around a vast kitchen table, sipping whiskey in fluorescent light as a generator rumbles outside. We are planning the next day's trek through the Kelabit highlands of Borneo, where Sylvester and his stoic friend, Tony, will guide us

"No, no that's OK," we answer. Jerry and I just want to see the jungle, far off-path.

The next morning, Tony shows up with a rifle and seven dogs.

"So we're going hunting?" Jerry asks.

"Maybe," Sylvester says.

And off we go, first rising through a plain of ferns and pitcher plants, then descending into jungle where the bushwhacking starts, amid huge trees rooted in six inches of sucking mud, with pointy branches, stabbing prongs, slashing vines, and thirsting leeches. I pause at times to snatch a few moments among the giants around me. I have no, absolutely no idea where I am or where we came from in this close, claustrophobic forest. There is no discernible trail. These guides are indispensable; I am at their mercy.

And yet Tony leads without ado, slashing our path, making his way as though he knew by heart every mud patch, every tree, every bloodsucker in this jungle.

How does a human being gain such keen awareness of his environment? And how does a population lose it?

Tony's dogs are kind and gentle beings. They follow us, then sprint ahead to lead, then back again to monitor our progress, sniffing us, making sure each of us finds the right way. They, as we, suffer the forest wrath with leeches between their toes and bugs buzzing across their backs. The trail smells of wet dog and sweaty humans.

We reach a bridge, a rickety log that breaks beneath a dog. He topples into the water, emerging sodden but quiet, and continues up the trail apace and unfazed.

There is a squealing ahead and—bam!—Tony is gone, sprinting through the jungle. The dogs have cornered a wild boar, and a few minutes later we find Tony on the hillside, hands upon a panting pig, bloody from a dog's nip. The boar struggles and stands to fight, but the animal is no match for Tony and his helpers.

"You are very lucky," Sylvester tells us. We were hunting, and the hunters have caught a pig, and we shall take it back to the village alive.

"Alive?" we ask.

"Yes, because we don't have the time." We have hiked all day. Darkness draws near, and there is no time to butcher here.

The pig blinks its eyes and breathes heavily on the ground as the two men tie its legs and stuff it into the expandable rattan backpack on Tony's shoulders. I look at the pig, it looks at me, and I grow misty-eyed. But why? It's a pig. I eat meat. This is how it works.

When it's cinched inside the basket, Tony wraps the nose and face tightly. The pig closes its eyes and Tony hoists the load upon his back.

"Heavy?" we ask.

"Not heavy," Tony says. Tony is a man of few words. Sometimes they are inaccurate.

We follow man and boar back to the village, stopping at one point briefly on the high banks of a small stream. In five minutes, Tony and Sylvester build a plank bridge with a bamboo railing using two machetes and supplies found within fifteen yards of where they build. We continue on through creeping nightfall and ever more mud.

We arrive in darkness. As I shower in cold water from a bucket, I smell burning hair—a familiar Asian scent—and I know the pig is no longer alive.

After I have dressed, I enter the house of Walter, Tony's brother. Walter sits on a four-inch stool beside the fire with a pig leg and a quarter of the animal's side. Piece by piece, he puts it into the fire to singe the hair and skin. Then he takes a cleaver to the hot flesh, shaving bristly singed hair onto cardboard spread across the floor. While he works, he talks of guiding, how to be a good guide. He says you must acquaint the tourists with the jungle, show them how to survive and what to eat and drink.

The pig is bloody, its inner workings visible. It all hangs out on Walter's floor. There's no separation here between pulsing animal and dinner on the plate. When Walter is through with the cleansing, he puts the leg in the sink and douses it.

"What do you do with the pig?" I ask.

"Cook it."

"How do you cook it?"

"Fry it." At times, Walter has no more words than Tony.

"The whole thing?"

"Yeah. And then we can take the bones for soup." He asks if I want to eat the meat fried with black soya. It's how they usually do it. Or else with curry. But tonight he has no curry.

Soya is just fine, I tell Walter. I get up close and look at the glistening red meat, just moments ago a pig in a basket. Walter sets it on a cutting board and slices the skin. He sections the meat, and blood runs everywhere. I can see the tautness of muscle in its leg.

I feel sorry for that pig, but my feelings are inconsistent. I've eaten pork all my life. Jerry and I had a pig roast at our wedding. And this pig led a completely natural existence in the jungle until its last three terrifying hours of life. How does that compare to America with factory-farmed pigs, raised in snug little cubicles, no room to roam, fattened to blue-ribbon proportions?

I remember visiting the state fair as a child, looking at all those pigs displayed, awaiting judgment, just to be sold and butchered. Pigs weighing half a ton. I never felt much in the way of remorse—they were pigs after all, and I was a girl growing up in Wisconsin. But I think about them now; are steel cages more humane than the basket in which our dinner was brought to its death?

Later that night, we head to Tony's yard, behind Walter's house. Several village men and hunting dogs have gathered around the fire, as ribs and backfat sizzle on the grill. Tony plays a cassette tape on his little boombox. It's a mix of old hits: "Nights in White Satin," "More Than Words," "Eye of the Tiger." He bought the tape in Miri, a town four hours by foot and one hour by plane from this barbecue in the jungle.

We listen to the music, and we all eat pig.

Right: Guide Tony Paran ties up a wild pig he captured with help from his hunting dogs in the jungles of the Kelabit Highlands.

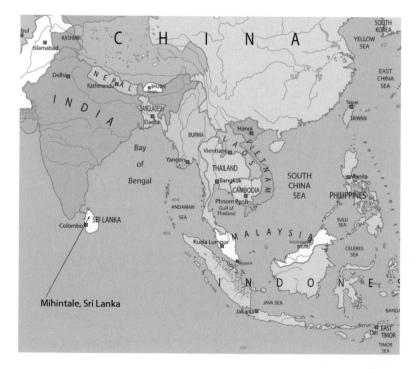
Mihintale, Sri Lanka

23. The Cradle of Wildlife - 2004

Our plane lands at midnight. There are few things more disorienting than landing in an unfamiliar city in an unfamiliar country at midnight. Our taxi motors past all-night tea shops, down empty streets, and through dark alleys south of Colombo as we search for a guesthouse that's supposed to be near the sea. It's 2 a.m. by the time we find it; we tumble straight into bed. We sleep—but not for long.

Sheeuk, sheeuk, sheeuk, SHEEUK.

Furious screeching wakes us in the wee hours: a ruckus so shrill it's impossible to rest. I stumble to the balcony and open the drapes. It's a zoo out there—crows and bulbuls, parakeets and flowerpeckers, squealing and flapping in the trees at the sun's first rays.

Jerry and I rise in a stupor of fatigue. We eat, we stroll the beach. A black-capped kingfisher sits on a wire; an egret naps with a cow. We see a black-rumped flameback, speckled koels, and dozens more parakeets with their rosy-ringed necks. It's our first morning in this fecund land—and we haven't even tried to find the wildlife yet.

Welcome to Sri Lanka.

In the month ahead we will see langurs and lizards, fox and mongooses, wild boar, snakes, chameleons, crocodiles, clouds of egrets, a herd of deer, black-necked storks, lesser adjutant storks, Asian openbills, Indian rollers, common hoopoes, so many peacocks, so many elephants. This is an island of diverse terrain, from dry, sandy beaches and coastal estuaries to evergreen forests and mountains that reach eight thousand feet. Such variety supports an abundance of life. It's not a big island, roughly the size of West Virginia, but more than 230 species of birds live here, as do 250 species of frogs. It's a panoply of life. But why?

"Because people don't eat them," says Ravi Corea, president of the Sri Lanka Wildlife Conservation Society. "Most people are Buddhist and they shy away from eating animals."

True—Sri Lanka differs from many of its Asian neighbors. We find no endangered animals (or their parts) in local markets. A young SLWCS volunteer named Maduranga tells me Buddhists in other countries behave differently from those in Sri Lanka. "They eat all types of animals, no?"

He is right: most Buddhist countries across Asia contain entire market sections devoted to meat—the usual pork and beef, but also snakes, turtles, wild cats, and bears. But Maduranga, like many Sri Lankans, eats only chicken and fish. He follows ancient mores that have guided his country for millennia.

*****

I learn on this trip that Sri Lanka is home to the world's first wildlife sanctuary. It's a place called Mihintale, which is still up and running since its inception in the third century BC. As the story goes, King Devanampiyatissa ("Tissa" for short) was hunting deer not far from the capital of Anuradhapura in the inland forests of Mihintale. "This was his hobby, killing animals," a Mihintale guide named Raju tells me. There on a mountaintop, Tissa came upon a visiting monk named Arahat Mahinda, the son of India's Buddhist Emperor Asoka. When Mahinda spotted the royal hunter, he called to him: "O Great King, the birds of the air and the beasts have an equal right to live and move about in any part of the island as thou. The land belongs to the people and all other beings; thou art only the guardian of it."

At that time there was no Buddhism in Sri Lanka. There was no thought that hunting was wrong. But Mahinda spoke of Buddhist ideals, which hold all life sacred and equal. He managed to convert the king, who decreed "no more hunting of animals." And with that, Tissa set out to persuade his subjects to follow the Buddhist way. He also declared Mihintale a wildlife sanctuary. Temples and shrines were built among the rocks, and today these ruins are known as the cradle of both Sri Lankan Buddhism and conservation.

Visit Mihintale now and you may glimpse the endemic Sri Lanka grey hornbill. You may find turtles and snakes; you may see a mother mynah attacking a lizard that tries to eat her young. You will definitely see primates, and probably a chameleon or two, as they sun themselves on trees the same color as their skin. And you will find the spot where Tissa met his converter: the rock on which Sri Lankan Buddhism and wildlife conservation converged.

It's a steep scramble up Mihintale's mountain, but railings and steps guide the way—unlike in Tissa's time. Up top, we catch wide views of the lowlands, vast tracts of paddies, and ancient reservoirs, called tanks, some of which date back centuries. Now, they burst with life. Fishermen in small wooden boats float among flocks of egrets and storks. Crocodiles swim these waters, and elephants come at dusk to drink and feed on nearby grasses.

As our travels unfold, we begin to see how Sri Lanka's archaeological sites showcase an ancient crossroads of religion and wildlife. Up the road a few miles we climb the steps to the Ruwanveli Seya, one of the country's most sacred spots. It's a massive white dome built more than 2,100 years ago and is thought to enshrine one of the Buddha's collarbones. On the surrounding esplanade, near the entrance, sits a human-sized slab of stone with ancient script. It is called the Inscription of Nissankamalla, a king who succeeded Tissa by 1,400 years. He prohibited trapping birds, killing animals, and fishing in the kingdom's tanks. He wrote that law on this hunk of stone, left intact today.

Down the road a few miles sits the Archaeological Museum in Anuradhapura. There, encased in glass, are tiny figurines shaped like a crab, a fish, and a tortoise. They were found in the waters around Anuradhapura, and they represent the protection of animals and sea life.

And then we find ancient urinals carved from stone. Our museum guide, Padama, explains that Buddhist monks designed them 1,500 years ago with the animals' best interests in mind. At that time, a monastery of 5,000 monks operated nearby, and all those men used the same plot of land for their daily, um, voidings. The land became acidic and unhealthy for the forest animals, Padama tells us, so the monks designed a squat toilet with an underground filtering system several layers deep. By the time the urine reached sand at the contraption's bottom, it was clean—and it didn't poison the nearby forest.

*****

We travel on a bit farther to Sri Maha Bodhi, and visit the world's oldest historically documented tree. It's a massive outgrowth of a clipping from the Buddha's tree of enlightenment, brought from India to Sri Lanka by Emperor Asoka's daughter. For two thousand years, its branches have sheltered and shaded living creatures. Today, thousands of worshippers visit the tree, praying beneath its shady reach, sharing the space with roosters and cats, egrets and orioles. Groundskeepers cart away barrel after barrel of flower and coconut offerings—so many tons in a given day—and dump them in a nearby bin. Presto: instant dinner for the many resident langurs.

I talk with an old man named Premaratna, who has traveled sixty difficult miles to pray for his ailing brother-in-law, a Buddhist monk. He adores this tree and thinks it sacred. "The Buddha gave to us," he says. Respect for life is the root of Buddhist scripture. And respect for animals dates to the Buddha's conception.

Legend says while the baby Buddha grew inside his mother, she dreamed of a white elephant in her womb. Astrologers took this as a sign of her fate to bear an exemplary human being. To this day, the elephant's eminence is woven in Sri Lankan tapestries and carved on society's walls.

But it's not just the elephant, it's all living beings. Through meals and conversations across the country, we learn this reverence for animal life extends to the dinner table, too. Corea tells me that to live and act without unnecessarily harming other creatures is called ahimsa. But it's more than a prohibition on killing. It means "entire abstinence from causing any pain or harm whatsoever to any living creature, either by thought, word, or deed." It requires a "harmless mind, mouth, and hand." These teachings are so ingrained in Sri Lankan Buddhist culture, he says, they help explain the island's preponderance of animals.

But then, why is Sri Lanka different from other Buddhist nations?

Corea points out that Sri Lanka has been Buddhist far longer than any other country. "Even India," he says. "India reverted back to Hinduism soon after the death of the Buddha." Sri Lanka does have a sizable Tamil population, the majority of whom are Hindus, but "the Hindu religion is very accommodating of other gods…since the fundamental belief in Hinduism is that all gods are a manifestation of the Brahma, the ultimate God." Hence, across the island, the two religions tend to mingle—though the people and their politics do not.

*****

For more than twenty years, Sri Lanka's Tamils in the north and east fought the Buddhist Sinhalese majority for independence. They call their proposed homeland on the north and east coasts of the island Tamil Eelam, and much of it lies in rubble when we visit. Twenty years of battle destroyed cities, homes, schools, hospitals. We see Sri Lankan army bunkers and bases across the north; we learn that many of the beaches and causeways are mined.

But the north also teems with wildlife. Bombed and potholed roads twist through groves of palms, flush with birds and more birds and butterflies, all hours of the day. Brahminy kites, cormorants, spot-billed pelicans, black-crowned night herons, little egrets, great egrets, grey herons, painted storks, black-headed ibis, red-wattled lapwings—we spot nearly every species in my handy Photographic Guide to Birds of Sri Lanka without even trying.

Jerry and I take a road trip one day, through the shimmering wetlands west of Jaffna. More birds, more sea, more marshes and swamps, more soldiers and guns, more barbed wire and checkpoints, more astonishing wildlife. One morning that week, Jerry sits on the balcony of our little hotel and there, in the trees among the debris, is an Asian paradise flycatcher, with its magnificent twelve-inch tail. Another day, south of Jaffna, Jerry stops to photograph a family of black-faced langurs jouncing through the foliage. He lifts his camera and a camouflaged man pops up from the brush. "No, no!" the soldier shouts, waving his arms. "Everything here is mined!" We retreat to the taxi.

*****

Sometimes in Sri Lanka, too much life competes for too little space. For years Corea and his group have worked to prevent conflict between people and elephants. We accompany him one long, hot day into the heart of Wasgamuwa National Park and the communities that surround it. The elephants have no instinctual knowledge of boundaries. They wander through nearby villages, trampling crops and destroying homes. In a single night, a single elephant can ruin a farmer's entire year. And every week in Sri Lanka, up to three elephants are killed in human-elephant conflicts. Were it not for traditional Buddhist beliefs, Corea says, that number would be higher. "There's still a lot of tolerance in these people." But it won't last forever. Eventually the people's Buddhist patience will crack.

Maduranga, the young chicken- and fish-eating SLWCS volunteer, understands the farmer's frustration. He comes from a village on the edge of Wasgamuwa. He tells me three bulls have tormented his neighbors repeatedly, and in one week alone, the elephants damaged eleven homes. "They always come to this village."

SLWCS is trying to prevent these attacks by building electric fences around villages to keep the elephants at bay. We travel along one such fence, a long line of hope for the villagers. It's a successful initiative so far. Elephant raids have greatly diminished, though sometimes the animals outmaneuver the people and break through.

Maduranga tells me of his conflicted feelings. He used to hate the elephants, but his job has helped him understand the animals and accept their natural tendencies. He has learned it takes profound patience for people to live in harmony with wildlife—just as Buddha taught twenty-five hundred years ago.

"When elephants come now, I am still angry," he says. "But not like before."

Right: An Oriental Garden Lizard scales a tree in Mihintale National Park. Buddhism originated in Sri Lanka in Mihintale in 247 BC, when King Devanampiya Tissa - on a hunting expidition - met Mahinda, the son of the great Buddhist emperor Asoka, and was subsequently converted.

23. The Cradle of WIldlife - 2004

Elephants from the Pinnawela Elephant Orphanage bathe in a river near the facility, part of the orphanage's daily routine. The orphanage began in 1975 as a home for baby elephants found abandoned in the wild. Now, other elephants found in distress are brought here, too.

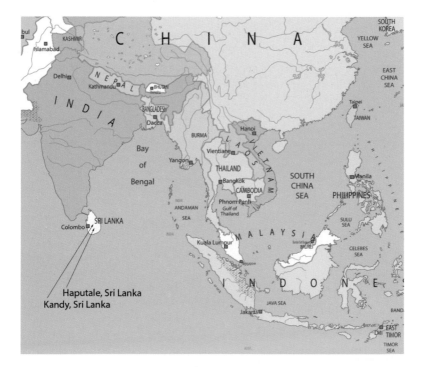

24. Journeys on a Tea Train - 2004

There is no reason to buy a first- or second-class ticket on the 8:55 a.m. train from Kandy to Haputale. A better ticket doesn't mean a seat. It only affords a more expensive chance to squeeze into the undifferentiated miasma.

We nudge our way into the snack car, packed to the walls with humans and their belongings. Every other car is full—people in the aisles, squatters in the corners, arms hanging from doors and windows. The train stands still. A soft rain patters across the tracks. The minutes pass. It's 9:15. It's 9:30. It's 9:45. No one is going anywhere yet.

At 9:55, precisely one hour late, we move. Jerry and I munch on "short eats," little fried spice rolls and dhal balls wrapped in newsprint and old receipts. These ubiquitous Sri Lankan streetside snacks will sustain us through this trip, though we don't know that now.

The only place to sit is a wet patch on the floor in front of the snack counter, beneath a missing ceiling panel. We've been warned of rain on this route. The manager of our Kandy hotel has told us about a downpour two days earlier that caused a "slight derailment" (which sounds to me an awful lot like being "kind of pregnant").

There is a powwow in the corner on the floor—two women and three girls eating dhal balls. A barefoot man, four feet tall and dressed in a sarong, passes through toting a basket of fritters with red onions and fried chiles.

[First stop.] We're only a few minutes down the tracks from Kandy. We seem only to gain more people, merging with the masses already on board. The snack bar does a decent business on cigarettes and hot cups of milk-thick tea, passed between arms and over our heads.

I watch egrets through the window as they feed in the paddies around us. It's nine days before Christmas and wild poinsettias are blooming on the hillsides, high and tall, in the lands where they grow naturally. It's beautiful out there, in a shroud of clouds and mists. Everything is luminous, everything is green. But everything drips with a never-ending dampness. My shower this morning did nothing to combat the turgid air, a sticky soup of smog and humidity. I'm coated in a familiar Sri Lankan slime.

[Stop: Gampola.] More passengers. No one exits.

This is a diverse car with the two of us among Tamils and Muslims and Sinhalese, and a woman from Holland on the floor beside us. Some people—tourists—take this train for the views of steep cliffs ribboned with tea plantations that abruptly end at dramatic drop-offs. Other people—locals—take this train to get from point A to point B cheaply. We hear of an observation car with upholstered seats—one per person!—at the end of this train. Supposedly, it has a glass roof and wide windows. But we hear all tickets were booked ten days ahead.

[Stop: Ulapane.] We chug on past sugarcane plots and olive palms, water buffalo and hills that disappear into layers of haze. We pass white dagobas and bodhi trees, just like the one where Buddha attained enlightenment. I've flipped over someone's backpack and I'm using it as a seat, my back hunched and body scrunched among six other legs that aren't my own.

[Stop: Nawalapitiya.] One Muslim family exits—but we mustn't gain hope. The conductor tells Jerry the crowding has yet to begin. Far more people get on than off from here on. The car will swell with humanity. Right now I count twenty-three people in this single car with two tables, two seats, and a grotty floor.

A wind starts with the train, but when we're stopped the air stands thick, damp, and oppressive. A man smokes against a closed window, the cigarette sending spirals against the filmy glass. Another man and his son board with lunch packets wrapped in newspaper. They claim a corner of one table, unfurl the paper, and dig their hands into the rice and curry. When finished, they stretch their arms out the window, rinsing their hands with a cup of water. Now a vendor makes his way through the cramped quarters, holding a basket brimming with peanuts and a tin of fragrant hot devil spice, Sri Lanka's answer to jerk seasoning.

We cross a crystalline stream with whitewater bends. The earth falls from view, straight down a cliff on our right side. Coffee berries hang from trees beside the tracks. Atop these hills: pines as they grow in Oregon. And all the way up the hillsides: rows of tea, waiting for pickers.

We've left people and houses and villages behind. It's all tea and hills and evergreens, with water and clouds draped over the highlands. The slopes almost glow with a type of plant that has foot long leaves, green upper sides, and the most vivid purple beneath.

We reach a tunnel and all goes dark except for the wispy light above us. Kids shout and whistle until we emerge to a view of waterfalls off the left-hand side. I no longer expect sights like these in Asia—so rare they are, when people give way to landscape. Huge slate boulders dot the hills. The tea, like cultivated acres of hedge. Miles and miles, a house or two, but mostly miles and miles of land. The British-era speed warning signs along the track say 15 km/hour, tops—9 miles an hour. That's optimistic.

[Stop: Galboda.] Jerry insists I take his spot by the door, where I can hang my head outside and await more spectacular views. I watch another train approaching and a great commotion as pedestrians scramble to get off the tracks.

I'm curious to see the designated third-class car, so I wander ahead. It's rammed with people on seats, babies on laps, more people in aisles, old men in dingy white sarongs and turbans squatting in the areas between cars. A man squashes through with a bushel of mangoes and a knife. Flick, flick. He peels one juicy yellow fruit for a customer.

Amid all this, the scenery never stops—steep hills, that lustrous green, a rain as though we're chugging through clouds. My ears begin to pop. As we inch higher and higher, the height of the vegetation drops. There are few tall trees but ever more terraces of tea carving the land.

I return to the snack car, and the mango man soon arrives—flick, flick, flick-

Scenes from the tea train between Kandy and Haputale in central Sri Lanka.

flickflickflickflickflick into a hundred little peelings. The slices go in a bag with chile salt sprinkled atop, handed to a group of Tamils in the corner. It's an art, cutting that mango. We can't resist. We buy a fruit, 10 rupees, 10 cents; it's tangy, fiery, and acidic.

[Stop: Hatton.]

A man with Canada written across his pack boards the train. "Is there room for another backpack here?" he asks, eyeing the woman from Holland, now standing.

"Ah, no. I was sitting," she says.

"You want to sit on my backpack then?"

"No, I'd like to sit on my pack," she says.

"OK. Well, I'm gonna have to put it somewhere." The Canadian drops his bag across our belongings, then briskly orders tea from a vendor out the window. He has just come from hiking Adam's Peak, a holy mountain which is said to have the Buddha's footprint on top. The Canadian says it's been raining all day, all night, and he's not pleased.

The peanut man returns. He tells the Canadian each bag is 10 or 20 rupees, depending on size. Mr. Canada thinks it's a rip-off. He thinks locals get more nuts for their rupees. But then he buys a bag anyway.

"I think Sri Lankans have it really bad," Mr. Canada says to Ms. Holland. "Because of the war. All the money went to the war, and now the war is over and the money should go back to the people—but it's not."

"There is a lot of corruption," she says.

He wants to go to Arugam Bay, to "do some writing," maybe a report on this situation. She tells him people need assistance from organizations such as the Dutch groups working here to help the elderly, orphans, and street kids. "They can't do it themselves so we have to do it for them," she says.

Within the month, Arugam Bay is destroyed in the tsunamis, and I think of Mr.

Canada, wondering where his journey has taken him.

We continue to climb, reaching the Summit Tunnel at 6,226 feet. The farther we go, the more brilliant the scene—drop-offs into oceans of fog; a forest of thick, old trees; another forest of painted gums with peeling bark in a rainbow of green and pink, white and yellow.

Something about the color of the clouds and the sky here reminds me of Crater Lake at the onset of fall, just before Oregon's rain turns to snow. A boy by the window points to a massive waterfall, flush from recent rains, a quarter mile wide. The whole car sways to that side as people angle for a view.

I sit on my pack atop a filthy floor, thinking about the price of a second-class ticket on all-day ride from Kandy to Haputale:

Seventy-nine cents.

24. Journeys on a Tea Train - 2004

Scenes from the tea train between Kandy and Haputale in central Sri Lanka.

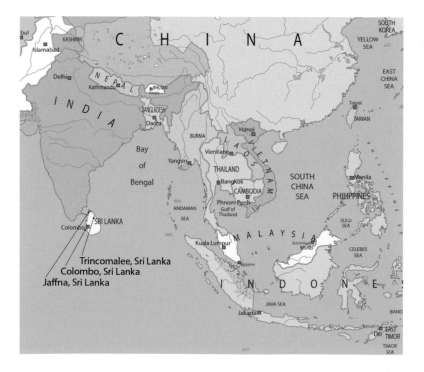

25. The Sea Before - 2004

Jerry and I traveled across Sri Lanka for the month preceding the 2004 tsunami that killed an estimated 275,000 people in eleven countries. We returned to our home in Thailand three days before the waves hit. Much of Sri Lanka was devastated.

Our visit to the country coincided with a cease-fire in a thirty-year civil war between the majority Buddhist Sinhalese government and the minority Hindu Liberation Tigers of Tamil Eelam (LTTE). That war ended in May 2009. But thousands of Tamil civilians remain in camps long afterward.

Jerry and I visited both south (predominantly Sinhalese) and north (predominantly Tamil) during our travels. In every corner of the country, Tamils and Sinhalese agreed: war would come again—and it did. Below are scenes from Sri Lanka's coasts, as they were in late November and early December 2004, just before the tsunami.

November 24, Colombo (south)

A storm comes. Black towers of clouds fade into a sheet of gray as lightning prickles distant rooftops. It comes, like most Asian storms, hard and fast. We dine tonight on the edge of the ocean in Mount Lavinia, just south of Colombo. We order devilled fish, chicken curry, and spicy rice. Two cats mingle with our feet and whine for scraps—feisty.

For a long while, we are the only people at this restaurant, so barren is this beach, a tropical beach with little hint of tourism. A couple of quiet men stroll through the darkened sand, talking and smoking, their silhouettes like mist. They have no light but the faint blip of a cigarette in the night air. A southbound train rumbles past, people cramped inside and spilling out the doors. The tracks follow the shoreline, closer to the water than any road. This place has the feel of a town abandoned after battle: roughened, empty, a little spooky.

November 25

This morning I talk with Marcus, the desk man at our guesthouse. He spent seventeen years in the navy, in the north and east, and he describes his combat days with the hallmark precision of a military man's tragic memory. "Our camp was attacked by LTTE in 1985. Third through fourth of May 1985. I was engaged in that face-to-face attack. We retaliated after forty-eight hours of attack." He remembers that three soldiers died and eight were badly injured—an amputated hand, an amputated leg, shrapnel wounds. After all these years, he still remembers the names of the dead and the cities where they had lived.

Marcus tells me he was excited to fight, not scared. He felt a duty to defend the lives of innocent people from "terrorist insurgents." He thought he would die in that attack. "I thought there was no way—I must sacrifice my life."

He admits the Tamils have not been treated kindly in the past fifty years; they suffered under the "Sinhala-only" law, which made Sinhalese the official language and gave the Sinhalese preference in jobs. "We must look at both sides." But warfare aimed at civilians—bombs and attacks in public places, a mark of the Tigers—is unconscionable, he says. "We must stop this nonsense."

*****

This afternoon, Jerry and I catch a train to Colombo. It takes thirty minutes in a shabby car with hard seats and hordes of people. The tracks skirt little shanties by the sea; there is nothing else on this stretch of coastline. Nothing but the poorest of homes, shacks huddled against each other and wedged between the rails and the water. Women bathe at communal spigots. I watch their eyes as we slowly bounce by.

We arrive at Colombo's main station amid hustle-bustle and riotous noise. A moaning, more like it. Buddhist monks occupy the sidewalk, chanting in unison, protesting the LTTE. They do not want a separate country, a monk tells Jerry. They want a unified Sri Lanka, Tamils and Sinhalese. So they sit and chant their story amid the frenzied rush of humanity getting on and off the trains. A platoon of police keeps an eye on them and the crowd.

We stroll around Colombo's seaside fort. It feels as though the war is not over. Snipers skitter atop skyscrapers; two wiggle and wave when we spot them from the street. All government buildings hide behind thick barriers of sandbags and concertina wire. A lone soldier peeks from an empty seaside lookout on a playground of rainbow-colored swing sets.

We pass bombed-out buildings, just the shells still standing; we pass others reduced to heaps of broken bricks. Again and again, police officers stop us and ask where we go—no problem to look around, they say, but no photos allowed. It's a nonsensical idea, trying to ignore what's plain for anyone to see. Colombo is under siege by an unseen enemy. Everywhere, even in the simplest actions, there is tension. A police post, sponsored by Coca-Cola, sits beside the Galle Face Green, the city's great promenade. There are checkpoints on the roads. A teenage couple carefully canoodles under a rainbow umbrella.

*****

It's Thanksgiving Day, we've almost forgotten. We drink beer at the Galle Face Hotel as the sun sets over rousing seas. Hotel construction workers pound behind us; the ocean pounds before us. A chipmunk visits, taking the fried spicy cashews I've propped on the leg of my chair. Crows cackle in the palms above us. The Indian Embassy stands within view; it is well guarded, like all others. Soldiers prepare for another storm, stringing a tarp over their rooftop perch beside a mounted heavy machine gun. The sky blackens, the sea turns slate, the air feels cool and good. The rain chases us inside as it pummels the banquet tables on the lawn, white cloths and glasses drenched. Hotel waiters in white shirts and black pants leap a low garden wall and sprint to retrieve the dishes.

*****

We return to Mount Lavinia that night by taxi. As we pass through the Tamil area of Bambalapitiya, our driver tells us Tigers are bad for business. "Tiger people are dangerous," he says. "They are suicide people."

I tell our driver we are from the United States.

"Ahh...Bush," he sighs.

I ask what he thinks.

If Bush had not been re-elected, he says, America would face more problems with Osama bin Laden. Al-Qaeda is a problem he understands—terrorists, he says, like the LTTE. How many times have the Tigers blown up hotels? Terrorists are bad for business, he repeats.

November 26

It's a Poya day, a Buddhist holiday, and the streets are bare. We head to a cramped little office in Bambalapitiya to buy LionAir tickets to Jaffna in the Tamil north. These days, the agent tells us, Jaffna is "more normal than Colombo," where every day brings a fresh murder or three.

LionAir resumed flights to Jaffna with the cease-fire in 2002, after a four-year hiatus. "Unfortunately," the agent says with a downward glance, "one of our planes was shot down." It happened in 1998. All forty-eight passengers and crew disappeared off the coast.

November 27, Jaffna (north)

We drop closer and closer to Jaffna, passing over sparkling estuaries. Emerald forests, egrets in rice paddies, red dirt roads, crisp air: it is beautiful, stunningly so. But the airport is a bunkered high-security zone. More soldiers, more encampments, more fences, more concertina wire, more glimpses of war. There is nothing to indicate it has stopped. This is Tamil Eelam, at the northern tip of the island.

The seventeen-kilometer road into town passes shot-up schools and bombed-out homes, businesses with nothing left, buildings with trees and bushes growing inside; for mile after mile every single human creation is destroyed. Most every corner in most every neighborhood is guarded by a Sri Lankan army bunker with soldiers watching.

November 29

We hire a van for a day trip, driving north and east, then back to Jaffna and west.

It's potholes all the way, nothing maintained. And everywhere, we see the Sri Lanka Army, the Sinhalese. Soldiers occupy the best beaches, Tamils tell us, and they've mined them all.

The young army soldiers we talk to admit they don't like it here. Tamils and Sinhalese living together, in fear.

These torn causeways wind through shady avenues of palms, past cows and goats, through wetlands full of rare and endangered avian life. I've never seen such winged creatures in such abundance. The birds, so light on their legs—they walk through minefields with peaceful feet.

The homes we pass were lovely and elegant in a previous time, perched on the property of retirement dreams. Before there were colonial art-deco villas set deep within coconut groves. Now there is nothing but shattered walls and missing rooftops. So many families vanished, and the contents of those homes have disappeared with them. We notice there aren't even squatters. Our driver says the rubble is often booby-trapped.

December 2

I'm sitting on our balcony in Jaffna. A cow swishes its tail across the street. People pass on bicycles and a small fire burns against a wall. The sun drips orange upon the bombed buildings around me.

We spend the day in a three-wheeled taxi driven by Mr. K, a newfound friend. He has a difficult past, having traded the life of a Tiger for that of a family man. All over Sri Lanka, men have been killed for the political thoughts he harbors: peace and normalcy, a future for his children.

Mr. K drives us to Kurikadduwan, where we board a ferry to Nainativu, a small island where Hindus and Buddhists meet. Amid five thousand Tamil villagers sits a Buddhist temple where the Buddha himself walked twenty-five hundred years ago. He came to Sri Lanka, ironically, to stop a war. Legend says he left his footprint here, which is why thousands of Sinhalese Sri Lankans make pilgrimages to this island. Hence, the government stationed a navy garrison here. The island's one paved road runs from the dock to the temple, and stops.

Just outside the temple is a navy bunker. A twenty-one-year-old army soldier

25. The Sea Before - 2004

Scenes along the waterfront in Colombo, Sri Lanka.

asks Jerry if he'd like to photograph his Russian-made RPD light machine gun. The soldier comes from the inland city of Kandy and has been stationed here six years. It's simple math to determine he was fifteen when he came to the island of peace with a weapon in hand.

Back on our balcony in Jaffna, the rain comes lightly from a heavy cloud over wavering sun. A clunky armored personnel carrier shuttles a load of soldiers up the road. A bus follows with more officers, then a truck. There has been rioting in Jaffna for the past two days. The circumstances remain cloudy, but it seems to be a squabble over fishing and money. Despite the rain of the past two days, it appears that the thunder jolts we've heard are grenades.

Mr. K has told us two boys died in the previous night's fighting. A curfew runs from 6 p.m. to 6 a.m., though we don't know whether it still stands. There is no news here beyond word of mouth. This afternoon, we hope to see an old ice factory, a five-story building on the coast, so Mr. K begins driving in that direction. The narrow road meets a cramped intersection crowded with people. We inadvertently find ourselves in the center of rioting, where the previous day's deaths occurred. The locals very politely advise us to leave—immediately.

December 7, Trincomalee (east)

This, known as Trinco, is a city on a bay, with islands and harbors, hills and fishing boats, birds and blue sky. It could be Seattle, but it's decidedly not. Trinco sits on gorgeous land buffered from the sea. But it shelters the worst ethnic hatreds and war mentalities on the eastern edge of Tamil Eelam. Buildings are barricaded and marked with skulls and crossbones. There is a decapitated statue of Gandhi on the main road. The town is a half-destroyed, half-abandoned wreck with no discernible center. As Jerry says, it's as though no one here gives a shit, yet the shit is literally everywhere. So is garbage, so are guns.

The owner of our guesthouse is a man named Tilko, a Tamil who came of age in London. There, he drove a taxi, washed dishes, and put himself through engineering school. He says his people are deeply united in their fight for freedom. "We are terrorists in the world's eyes. But the people have suffered."

Tilko returned during the cease-fire to help rebuild. He has opened several hotels, north and south, but he waits for lasting peace to pursue his grandest visions—he wants to build a resort on a small seaside plot outside Jaffna, and another one here, facing a coral island that's good for snorkeling.

But not yet.

Now, it is time to live with war on the mind. Tilko plants rice and bananas on his vacant lands. Fields can be replanted after they are shelled. When he works on his hotels in town, he buys only cheap (though tasteful) materials because he knows the building may not last. "If there is war, we have to rebuild."

Jerry and I take a taxi to the nearby tourist beach of Nilaveli. Our driver turns down a dirt trail and there it is, big wide sand, a few men casting lines, and nothing. An abandoned hotel, no restaurants, no tailor shops or tattoo stalls. It's what happens when paradise goes to war.

A few scattered hotels lie farther up the road. We stop at a place where, for seventeen dollars, you can rent a basic room with a porch overlooking the ocean. The pool-in-progress hasn't seen workers in years. A military bunker lurks next door. There are no guests when we visit, but the manager assures us business picks up in spring.

December 26, Thailand

A tsunami strikes Asia, killing 275,000 people or more. Hardest hit are Indonesia, Thailand, and Sri Lanka.

Early January

The little hotel we visited in Nilaveli is gone; we read about it in updated online guidebooks. "Flattened," "totalement detruit," "completamente distrutto." Much like the streets we strolled in Trinco, where the waves unearthed landmines and scattered them across what was left of town. Much like the tracks south of Colombo, where the tsunamis killed at least eight hundred on a southbound train. That train was called the "Queen of the Sea."

*****

A week or so after the tsunamis, an envelope arrives from Mr. K. "I pen this letter to remember you. I and my family are in good health," he writes. But northern Sri Lanka is not. Mr. K sets off around the Jaffna Peninsula, to help where he can, to do what millions of Sri Lankans have hoped to do for decades: rebuild and renew.

Evening view of downtown traffic in Jaffna, Sri Lanka.

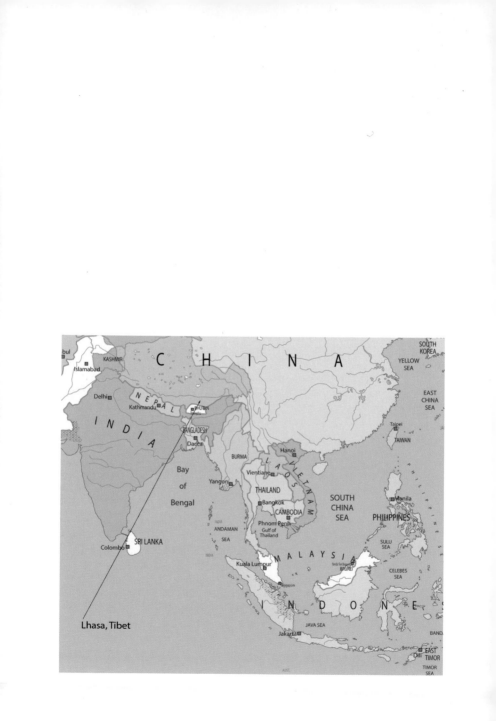

26. Tibetan Diary - 2000

I'm sitting on the crown of the world with the Potala Palace straight ahead, looking like a postcard. Prayer flags flutter in a dry breeze across a maze of rooftops, where women have set kettles on small metal stands to warm with the aid of little solar reflectors. All around, up above, are cocoa brown peaks that sprawl into distant snowflecked shards of rock that continue on toward more ice-laden wonders of the world. Glaciers spill into falls that tumble to this plateau, where almost all major Asian rivers originate—the Indus, Yangtze, Yellow, Mekong, Brahmaputra, Karnali, Sutlej, and Salween. So much of the world drinks of Tibet.

In the ancient part of town, cobblestone corridors lead to whitewashed homes, cheered with bright blue flowery trim around the windows and potted flowers growing on the sills.

The streets are choked with vendors offering yak wool, yak steak, yak butter, and bricks of tea. Tall men with long, dark braids and red headbands mosey through the alleys. Two such men fancy Jerry's camera, and they exchange looks and glances while roughly examining the contraption as it hangs from Jerry's neck.

There are men and women in green robes, brown robes, yak fur, shiny silk, beads, bangles, strings through the ears, bright striped aprons, rosy cheeks, and embroidered lapels. There are faces with long noses, short physiques and the bodies of big, muscular herders. Pilgrims waddle through town, buying, selling, looking, absorbing the scene. And where the cobblestone ends, everything shifts from Tibetan to Chinese: the whitewash turns to tile; the buildings from intricate works of craft to square concrete boxes; the roads from pokey and narrow to wide and rushing.

For better or worse, the contrast is visible in the countryside, too. It's more than sixty miles between the airport and Lhasa; we pass clear waters and goats and yaks and men and women living pastoral lives. We also pass Chinese bridges and Chinese workers and Chinese smokestacks and Chinese high-rises-in-the-making.

*****

Qi has a little shop in Lhasa. He comes from neighboring Gansu province and feeds us spicy Muslim food from home—cucumber salad, hot and sour soup, and rice. Qi wants to live in the United States, and he probes us on matters of money and passports and flights and salaries and all the particulars that would influence his dream of making it big with a Muslim restaurant in America. That's what he intends to do. "After two years, I will have some money and I will go and make a restaurant in America and make a fortune," he says.

Qi is looking for help from westerners wherever he can find them. Jerry hands him a business card; Qi examines it, then asks if he can write to us. Yes, we reply. He asks us how much it would cost to send a letter from the United States to China. I tell him maybe a dollar. He says he pays twice that much to send an envelope the other way.

He asks how much food would cost in America. We look at our plates and say around seventeen dollars. He's surprised, or dismayed, or both. Then he begins a lengthy barrage of questions: How much to fly to the States? How much to start a restaurant? How much would he earn as a chef? How long could he stay in America? How long can we stay in China? How much did we pay to fly to China? Do we need a "people's card" to visit China? How much, all in all, for him to go to America?

These are questions we cannot adequately answer, but no matter. Two years, he says, and he will have the money. He is confident. But can we help him?

We tell him he can write to us and we'll do what we can, but the government decides who gets in and who doesn't, and we are powerless in such decisions. Qi likes our answer anyway, and says he'll write to us. And then he implores us:

Return to his restaurant as soon as we can—for noodles.

*****

We visit the Jokhang Temple, the most sacred of all in Tibet. People come from every pocket of the country, hitching rides in the backs of trucks and enduring days of bumps and bruises, cold and snow, the dangers of icy roads on cliffs— just to worship at this temple. They land in Lhasa and stay for two months, prostrating themselves in this holy place. All day, and late into night, all across Lhasa, pilgrims bow and kiss the earth with their prayers.

And all across Tibet, they walk and twirl their prayer wheels in the perambulatory circles they make around temples. The wheels never stop. Each revolution is a prayer in itself. It's as though twirling were a natural part of human life, of breathing and sleeping. Each wheel contains a mantra, carved in Sanskrit. On Lhasa's streets, we see craftsmen chiseling the metal wheels that hold those holy words. Tap tap tap. An artist works on his stoop, with a cigarette dangling from his mouth. A young boy beside him watches carefully, learning the ancient, sacred trade.

We shop. We buy a bag full of saffron and a horseman's stirrup for a friend who likes to ride. We buy a little silver vessel, three cones of tightly packed tea leaves, a turquoise bead for Jerry's sister, and two cans of Chinese-brewed Pabst for my mother, who worked as a young woman in the original Milwaukee factory. For all of these gifts we are forced to bargain as a woman clutches my arm in one hand, a calculator in the other, and demands to know our price.

*****

Our guide, DJ, says he will take us to try chaang, a barley beer known as the nectar of the gods. We pile into a bus and he directs the driver this way and that way across the dusty town. He knows of a special place where locals go for the drink. He's never been there, he says; most people brew their own. But he is sure this is the spot for us to sit and sip.

We arrive at a wide grassy field full of large, colorful tents on the outskirts of Lhasa. Inside, on worn mats, are several small pillows where we can rest our rumps. A seventeen-year-old girl brings a green soda bottle to the center of our circle and pours its cloudy contents into the individual juice glasses before us.

She makes sure each glass stays full to the top the entire time we sit. The mild brew sends warmth through our systems. All is calm, but only for a moment.

Our presence quickly attracts a ragged, cheery, respectful crowd. One old woman plops herself in the corner, guzzles a bowl of brew, then sticks her tongue out in a customary sign of respect. Next, a guitar player strums a long, carved wooden instrument painted red, blue, and green. He serenades us; we listen, then offer a small tithe. And when we do, another guitarist comes with a singer. Then another. Soon they all come, hands stretched and eyes pleading. "They are Tibetan beggars," DJ tells us. We finish the bottle of chaang, pay our share, and struggle to reach the bus amid a swarm of arms.

This is a rambunctious place, DJ says. The locals get riled up when they drink. Tibetans, he explains, are a fighting bunch, women included. This prairie of chaang tents rumbles when Chinese patrons come in their jeeps. The liquor takes hold, and the fights begin.

*****

We meet a few travelers, and together we hire a driver to take us into the open— across the great plains and over steep passes that are this land.

Our driver is Neema; his name means "sun." He helps me find and buy a can of oxygen in case the altitude gets to my head, which it already has. We spent the previous couple of days stumbling around Lhasa trying to acclimate gasping lungs and aching brains before heading to higher grounds. Neema's big beast of a vehicle is an old Toyota Land Cruiser. Jerry sits in the way back, where the gas fumes hurt more than the bumps. But he gets a wide view of the valley, and its ripples of permafrost, and the dotted marks of yak prints, and the towering skyward-pointing slopes—a scene that more than makes up for sore buttocks and noxious air.

We ride through tiny farm towns, far from one another; the school walls in these places are painted in bright red Chinese characters that pronounce the merits of education. This I learn from a fellow traveler, a Cantonese-speaking woman named Helena from Hong Kong who is here with her Finnish husband.

We head toward the Drigung Monastery, an eight-hundred-year-old meditation center that clings to the mountainside at thirteen thousand feet. Giant birds circle overhead when we arrive. In Tibet, the sky is a sign of life and death. When a person dies, the body is served on a mountaintop to the giants of the sky—raptors as tall as small humans. It is possible to know when and where a burial occurs simply by following patterns of flight. The air swells with birds that circle and swoop, showering the world below with the whoop, whoop, whoop of their massive wings. The aim is to return the human shell—the body—quickly, naturally, to the earth so the spirit can move into another life.

Our Hong Kong companion tells us southern Tibetans do something similar in water, offering bodies as food for the fish. But criminals, she says, are buried in soil, where their bodies take years to decompose in this high, arid land. It is punishment, "a long wait for new life."

I lie here in our shared dorm room on a ratty old mattress atop a slat bed, my book atop a weathered orange pillow. Neema drinks tea and chats with another man in the corner. The window beside this bed opens directly to a view across the valley we crossed to get here. The mountain beyond reaches fifteen thousand feet at least, its peak packed in white, with prayer flags rippling in wind. The sun shines now after a light snowfall that swiftly evaporated.

*****

Come morning, we hurry for the road with a long day's journey ahead. Pink alpine light turns the mountaintops neon white, the moon still shining, the air cold and crisp. The Toyota traces a frigid river before meeting vast open plains.

At one point, in the apparent middle of nowhere, we stop the Land Cruiser to talk with a couple of goat herders and the young girl trailing along with them. The land is dotted with lumps of snow and frozen mud. The trio travels with some two hundred goats and a fancily clad horse with matted, icicled fur. We learn that one goat can fetch up to three hundred yuan in Lhasa, making the herders' lot worth more than seven thousand dollars—a local fortune.

We share oranges, crackers, chocolate wafers, and hard candies with our weathered friends. One of the men asks Jerry for the remaining Sprite in his bottle—flat after its fizz released in this atmosphere of low pressure. The herder takes the bottle anyway, in exchange for a wide smile.

Farther along the road, we meet a mountain pass in a blustery wind. We eye a truck heaving its way up the other side. It fails and fails again—though somehow we manage to maneuver our way to the top, where prayer flags flap in a spray of sleet. The other side leads to Namtso, one of the world's highest saltwater bodies, at 15,500 feet. Yaks and goats and herders and tents dot the vast plain, shrouded in a veil of white weather.

Neema remarks, as we traverse this mountainous journey over ruts, lurching through mud ravines, that the many full trucks we see heading into Lhasa, and the empties heading out, result from an incredible imbalance in trade. China sends its goods to Lhasa, but Tibet, he says, has nothing to trade in return.

*****

The day wanes quickly, and so does the light. A wind kicks up curtains of snow, obscuring the views we've had all day. We settle into a cold, spare room beside the lake, seeing little of the vast frozen body out there. Everyone gathers in the community room next door, where a few other travelers congregate for yak-butter tea, talk, and the promise of warmth from an inadequate and underperforming yak-dung stove.

Later, we return through shocking cold and dark to our unheated room. The sky has cleared and we can see the lake with little ice floes jutting from a blue-white sheen. The faint remains of a faraway sunset leave pink, vertical streaks connecting earth to sky. A nearby goat herder hoots and snaps at his animals as they clamber among nearby rocks, lively and seemingly impervious to the bone-snapping cold. A hawk swooshes its wings overhead, slicing thin air.

*****

In daylight, we meet a woman who lives in a cave, just a short walk from the nearly warm guesthouse kitchen. She has red-framed windows and doors across the cave's wide opening, and inside she has turned the little nooks and crannies of rock into living spaces. The nun is short and somewhat hunched, and she wears the maroon cloth of a monk. She welcomes us into her home behind several large boulders and a string of prayer flags. One dark room is her temple, with a golden Buddha up front and a stool where she sits and studies Buddhist texts. A brighter room serves as her kitchen. We donate a little cash to her temple. Then she shows us her flashlight and points to the battery chamber. I dig four Duracells from my bag and hand them to her. She beams with delight.

This woman's little abode opens onto a sandy, rocky expanse that fronts the lake. And when the air clears, she has unobstructed views of distant peaks that rise to twenty-one thousand feet. That string of mountains reflects and sparkles across the water.

*****

We leave Namtso in a small caravan of travelers in Land Cruisers—safety in numbers, the drivers explain. And it's a good thing. Just an hour out on the expansive plains, the Toyota stalls in a river. We stop and await our comrades. I meet a young woman collecting yak dung along the icy water. We speak to each other in our respective languages, understanding little but intuiting much. I touch her white sack and see the hardened brown lumps. She tells me she burns them for fire—just as our hostess at Namtso did, piling more and more crumbling poo-pies into the cookstove that heated our water, prepared our sweet butter tea, and kept us warm as the sun set and rose again.

I peek beneath the young woman's thick yak parka and peer at her green Western-style tennis shoes. We laugh. Together, we stomp through the mud, which slurps against our feet and sticks to our soles, and we laugh again. We angle toward the Toyota, now surrounded by the other travelers and drivers. A blue truck is now tethered to our vehicle by one strand of rope. When it naturally breaks, the drivers tangle several strands together in an effort to increase the rope's strength. I learn, here in the mud, just before our mountain ascent, that the Toyota's four-wheel drive doesn't work. "Not good," I tell my dung-collector friend as we watch the blue truck revving. The Toyota lurches forward a bit, then settles again into its mucky rut.

Finally, after ten minutes more of tug-and-rock, it moves. We pile into the Toyota and I dig through my backpack for an orange and some candies for my friend. She smiles, and we go our separate ways. She returns to her postcard land, wearing her yakskin coat lined in fur, carrying a burlap bag full of poop, hiking across short, stubby grasses in tennis shoes.

*****

Just before we reach the pass, at seventeen thousand feet, the Toyota stalls. It's not surprising as we have been plowing through two feet of fresh snow atop ice atop the dirt road for some time now. Neema starts the motor again and slips and slides on the ice, not going forward, but perceptibly going sideways, toward the edge of a cliff. We travelers flee the vehicle and observe from a distance. The rest of our caravan joins us, and we learn that not a single driver among them has a shovel, an axe, or any tool that could be used to dig a trench. Suddenly the sky turns white and little flurries begin to fall. Neema mentions something about a Buddhist sort of que sera sera, a belief that whatever will be, will be— based on religious grounds. The road, the cliff, driving, falling.

Jerry believes in physics, and starts digging wheel paths with his hands. He is quickly joined by the other male travelers, and in twenty minutes the jeep is again sliding through the snow, away from the cliff.

*****

Back in town, safely, we eat a late dinner with our fellow travelers at a place called the Lhasa Kitchen. We talk of many things, but most notably "the Tibet issue." Helena tells us what she learned of Tibet in school, in Hong Kong. It is not at all what we learned or what we proclaim to know as Americans. She gives us the official Chinese line, taught nationwide, that Tibet belonged to China long ago until the Qing dynasty, poor and weak, lost the territory. Tibet then became a pawn for Britain and India, she says. In the 1950s China sought to re-unite its long lost branches. They say the invasion was a liberation that restored this remote land to its rightful place in the Chinese world.

*****

Our guidebook mentions a couple of Lhasa restaurateurs who help needy children. The book suggests pens and paper as appropriate gifts, so we take a bag of items to the restaurant. The owner eyes me suspiciously.

"From who?" she asks.

"From us," we say.

We end up meeting her husband, and the four of us share long, deep discussions about Tibet. The husband explains that the couple previously worked with an orphanage that was closed a few years earlier. The head lama went to the United States, to raise money; he returned to arrest and imprisonment in China. "We don't know what he said… he must have said something." The government closed the orphanage and returned the kids to their home villages.

The couple tells us they must be careful. Their phone lines are tapped. People are watched. They ask how we heard of them. When we answer that our guidebook talks of their work, she says she cannot talk about it.

Everything in town is politics, he says. But things are different for the nomadic Tibetans. "They know nothing about politics. They don't know how to read... they don't know about paperwork...they know nothing about independence."

I ask whether the nomadic life has changed under the Chinese, and he says no. The people are so far from Lhasa, the center of social life. They roam, they graze, just as in the old days. "The government doesn't care about that," he says. The government only cares what comes from people's mouths in town. People can think, he says, but the authorities are "very sensitive" to what is said.

I ask him what life would be like without the Chinese, and at first he laughs. "There should be a transition." Tibetans don't have the education or leadership skills to run their own country, he says. Neither do they like taxes. Little is produced here. We talk of the full trucks coming into Lhasa and the empty trucks going out. Tibet has little to trade. "Tourism is the only source of income," he says.

We talk of Holiday Inn, which closed the best hotel in Tibet in 1997 because, she says, "they said all the money was going to the Chinese." Which was mostly true. But the decision to leave has hurt the economy. Tibet's only luxury hotel gave locals the chance to wait tables, work the front desk, manage money and business. "They were learning so much."

*****

I meet two young women sitting cross-legged in a dank room of the nunnery where they live. Their job is to make little prayer spools. One hands a thin strip of paper to another, who slaps the paper onto a woodblock, presses it with a roller, flips the paper onto a stack, then re-inks the block. Each print is wrapped snugly around incense, then cinched with silk. This repetitious pattern continues from 9 a.m. to 6 p.m.

One of the women tells me she is twenty-two and has lived here for ten years.

Her companion is twenty-six and she, too, has spent the previous decade as a Buddhist nun. They work throughout our chat. Only at complicated questions or for quick lessons in English do the women momentarily pause from their work.

The younger nun was born in a village outside of Lhasa, but her family now lives in the city. She has three brothers and three sisters; one of each lives in India. The others she sees frequently. I ask how long she will stay in the nunnery, and I am at first confused by her answer, which sounds like "today" or "two days." But what she's really trying to say is, "until I die." She thanks me for helping her with English.

I ask her why she came to the nunnery. This time, her answer is immediately clear to me:

"For the next life."

She asks me: "What do you think of your country?"

I tell her some things are nice and other things are not so nice.

Nice—the word itself is confusing, but the meaning of the sentence she understands. She tells me: "I think your country is very good because it is a democracy. Tibetans like democracies. Tibet is not a democracy."

I ask both women whether Tibet would be better without the Chinese. They don't understand my word "better," but they do understand when I replace it with "good."

"Yes, yes," they answer together. "We hope the Chinese will go back to their country."

Are China and Tibet separate countries? "Separate" throws them off, but "different" does not.

"Yes, yes," they answer again.

Was Tibet good before the Chinese came?

"Yes, very good."

Our conversation continues amid the pat pat pat of their work.

How do Chinese people treat Tibetan people? "Treat" is confusing, so I rephrase: Are the Chinese good or bad to Tibetans?

"This one we cannot answer because some are very good and some are bad. But the Chinese government is bad." Also: "We have no freedom." The younger nun says she likes America because America is free.

Do you like China? I ask them both.

Slap slap slap.

"Not so beautiful," the elder woman answers amid the rhythmic assembly line that turns wisps of paper into eternal prayer.

Left: An innkeeper greets the morning with Buddhist prayer beads in one hand and a steaming cup of yak-butter tea in the other on the shores of Namtso Lake.

26. Tibetan Diary - 2000

Monks and laypeople carry a new Buddha statue up the footpath leading to the Drigung Monastery in rural Tibet. The monastery clings to a mountainside at nearly 13,000 feet above sea level.

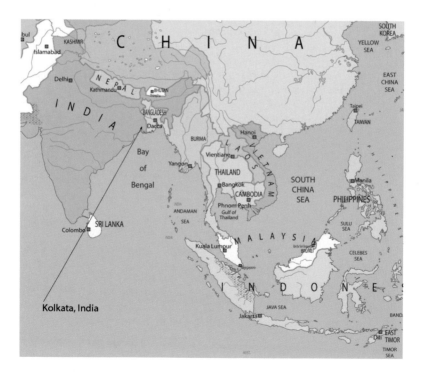

Kolkata, India

27. Stuck in Kolkata - 2007

I remember a vast sea of darkness as the plane descends over the Bay of Bengal just before 1 a.m. So much fog, so little light—I feel smothered. The lights outside Kolkata flicker faintly as we approach. But mostly, everywhere, there is darkness where a city of 16 million people should be.

Jerry greets me at the airport. He took an earlier flight, and he's already made a friend—the kind and reliable driver of a yellow Ambassador taxicab, which flies through the streets to reach our hotel. People sleep everywhere, beneath tarps, covered in cloth, sprawled across wooden carts in the medians. Irregularly placed streetlamps ooze an irregular orange light that hardly illuminates. Lumps of bodies big and small, kids and adults. Dogs prowl the alleys, licking garbage. Cows curl beside the road. More bodies, more bumps of humanity laid to rest for one night. Like every night, I suppose—entire streets full of people sleeping without walls.

Jerry looks whipped when I see him, as though he's climbed to the mountain-top and faced a lashing wind. So much humanity, he keeps saying. It's hard to fathom. We've lived and worked and traveled in Asia for a decade. But India, to us, is new.

Just as we open the door to our room, around 2 a.m., children clamor through the street chanting as a young man thumps on a drum. They wave and smile, sing and shout, stomp and clap, and proceed on their merry middle-of-the-night way. "It's overwhelming," Jerry says. All of it.

The next day we wander until we are too tired to continue. The incessant daytime clamor of color, noise, and light is a marked contrast to my dark introduction to India the night before. There's a constant honking, a swarm of yellow cabs sharing the cobbled pavement with barefoot rickshaw runners, dogs and goats, cats and mud. We drink tea at a stall that offers tiny clay cups. It's like sipping from mini flower pots, which lends a dusty, earthy beginning to the sweet milky drink. When finished, the cups get dropped. The streets are littered with shards, which are swept and ground into the street, back into the earth from which they came.

We stop for a snack—not to sate a hunger but to occupy an empty table in the back corner of a small restaurant where fans swirl the melting air and the cacophonous street stays thirty feet away. I have no appetite, not after all that tea and a moist piece of cardamom barfi, plus our breakfast of fish curry and rice. But I order anyway, coffee with an onion vada dosa. Yum. A crispy paper-thin pancake stuffed with shaved raw onion, served with thin curry and a curd for dipping. I savor, while the world spins and heaves outside the shop door.

It's so much for the eyes and ears. So much population in every direction. Colors and smells, constant movement. Noise. So much noise.

There is so much action and motion, but little evidence of creation: almost nothing here is new. Colonial brick buildings crumble around their inhabitants. Age-old sidewalk pumps offer water for washing and brushing teeth. Tea shops abound, on every street—but nothing like a Starbucks to be found. Internet is relatively scarce. Stuffy little shops crammed with people all vying for use of a few shared computers. I suddenly feel acutely out of touch, and far away. But from whom? From where? Life here is a swarm of millions. Can such masses be out of touch?

A man by the market insists I try "Indian water ball," a small puff of pastry, hollowed out and filled with potatoes and a spiced watery soup, cool and peppery.

There is tea everywhere except when we want it, except when we look. We take the tram to Howrah Bridge the next morning, then walk and walk, half searching for caffeine, but fully agog at all the sights. Men bathe on the sidewalk at spurting fountains; they scrub clothes and bodies alike on the blackened ground. There is light, amazing beams of light, dawning upon narrow alleys and gardens. Decrepit British-era apartments house ornate inner-sanctum courtyards that collect the day's amazing rays. Men sit reading newspapers in the rare quiet within. Look through the gate, through the looking glass, through the rabbit hole, and into the Raj.

We do find our tea eventually, in a corner shop, two men, and just a cupboard of a room. The master sits on the upper shelf, his helper below. The assistant occupies a space about 5 feet long, 4 feet wide, and 3½ feet high. There, he squats by a fire that boils the tea he serves. He taste-tests by putting one single drop on his left palm and popping it into his mouth. Then the same with sugar, only that he smacks to his forehead—I have no idea why. To sweeten his thoughts?

All across this city, men huddle and work in offices this size. Slots. Cubicles. Closets. Holes. They sew pants, make tea, sell cigarettes; all from a few square feet. The men who sit and work low to the ground have developed a means of squatting that brings the knees straight out to the sides but the feet tucked beneath the butt. It must take years to learn.

The market clock chimes on every hour like church bells. Crows scour the streets, squawking and watching from perches in Kolkata's trees. Rickshaws jingle with the bells their drivers wear. And taxis, too many to count, honk at everything, absolutely everything, all the time.

Dizzying. That's what Kolkata is. Over the days, I stand on street corner after street corner, it doesn't matter which or where. And I wonder, how do people live this way? How, among the unflagging movement and chaos and grit and noise and color and unpredictability? I begin to think that in Kolkata, noise is fuel. I think of Indians who leave and visit the Grand Canyon or Yosemite or Glacier Park. Do they fear or detest the silence? It must haunt their ears. When one grows up amid incessant commotion, what does silence do? Perhaps it feels inhuman to live without the scent, the touch, the heartbeats of others against the skin.

Mother Teresa's Home for the Destitute and Dying stands small in the shadow of Kalighat, temple of Kali the Destroyer. The home's ornate structure is set among minaret-like spires and dilapidated brick buildings along streets clogged with people who have nothing—nothing material.

The men and women of the streets look no different from those inside Mother Teresa's home—except those inside get cots and the gentle stroke of glove-clad volunteers who massage their wafer-thin bodies. There is some controversy over Mother Teresa, her stance against abortion, her assertions that suffering is life and God would provide—amid endless waves of death on India's filthy streets. But who criticizes? Foreigners half a world away? A full world away? More than a world away? Let them come here and take a look, then offer a solution to the problem of India's dying.

Just a short walk away is Babu Ghat, a temple on the water. It is both a holy place and a practical place, for praying and bathing. People gather on the steps leading to this wretched canal, steps lined with human hair, little curls that have been shaved from young men's heads. The chunky brown-green waters swirl around human hands and feet as dozens bathe. A woman washes another woman's hair. A man sits on the bottom step, lathering his body, then dipping into the water. Another man stands shoulder deep, head bowed and hands clasped in prayer. The air is the same muddy color as the water. Farther out: boats and barges trudge through the canal, spewing smoke, bumping into something heavy bobbing just below the surface. A cooling breeze blows as crows hop about a trash heap, slowly sliding into the river. Kids swim with glee. People arrive with little cups and plastic canisters, which they fill with murky water to take home. They respect this river as their ancestors did.

*****

I sit now beneath a rumbly old air conditioner as horns honk outside my window. I have showered, I still stink. My nose blows black. Yet my heart slows and a restfulness fills my body as I write while sitting alone in the middle of this king-sized bed. I have never before been so flabbergasted, so lost in how to describe a place.

It is madness. And yet people are unfailingly kind. Of a thousand we pass in a minute or two, there are no insults or scowls. And there are thousands, literally, who pass every minute; a rush of human beings so strong and heavy a person could be trampled if she stops. But if she does stop and lies on the pavement, she may sleep soundly, as many do by the train station. Some even appear dead— sprawled motionless as porters rush past with loads on heads, and the higher classes with shopping bags in hand, and the dogs and kids and taxis and rickshaws and bicycle carts. None of that stops. But the masses part around those sleeping on filthy ground amid the endless zoo of noise.

The human river flows up the stairs and over the Howrah Bridge, a raised steel gully of traffic passing left and right. Below, boats shuttle yet more people back and forth through cloudy blue-gray waters. Parked barges await loads of who knows what for who knows where. Crows zigzag the air between two banks, and higher up, hawks circle this stewing, streaming earth.

Across the way is a flower market. Down, down, down we pad the steps, then halt in our tracks amid yet another cacophony of color and life; of marigold mounds and people selling them; of space so cramped that humans grab each other, squishing together and holding tight when trucks roll through. Up and down go the hillocks of orange and yellow flowers; all around go the feet and bodies. A hole is cut into the brick wall separating this chaos from the railroad tracks, whose stench seeps straight into the flowers. Men squeeze through the hole to piss on piles of garbage.

Here among the flowers we find puchka. Water balls, just as we had before, but different because of the setting. Street food is entirely defined by its setting.

A man in the middle of this muddle sells the little semolina dough balls, hollowed out and filled with mashed potatoes mixed with black salt, roasted cumin, and red chile, then doused in water with tamarind (or green mango or lemon) and masala spices. But I can't even get up next to the vendor to see his selections. Too many people.

Across the tracks lies an intersection that clogs with buses, trams, trucks, taxis, rickshaws, and human runners whose job it is to shuffle goods atop their heads back and forth across the bridge. The porters move faster than stalled traffic, jogging on bare feet, toting bamboo baskets of potatoes. Other men lug heavy carts across the road—running, running, all day long.

Most people here have no toilet, no home with water, and so they gather by the dozens, by the hundreds, on street corners where public pumps pour forth and men lather their bodies while crouching in the gutters. Others immerse themselves in the Hooghly, the same river that collects and flushes the detritus of Kolkata. Public bathing is an ancient habit, born long before diesel fuel, oil slicks, chemical waste, and people in such great masses. Still, Kolkatans carry forth, living in many ways largely as they have through history. Are there many in Chicago who live exactly as their grandparents did? Are there many in Kolkata who do not?

27. Stuck in Kolkata - 2007

A view of a common neighborhood in Kolkata, showing buildings, vehicles and people's clothing that have little changed in 50 years.

We meet a man on the street. We are walking to breakfast and he is walking to work at a shop on the Esplanade. Our paths converge.

"India is very big," he says. First words to us.

"Kolkata population 20 million." That might be a little high, but perhaps not. He asks, "What do you think of Kolkata?"

"It's very interesting," I tell him. And Jerry asks the man, "What do you think of Kolkata?"

"I am born in Kolkata so everything is the same to me." He asks where we're from. "United States. Population: 300 million," he says. People here are keenly aware of size and space. It takes the man exactly twenty minutes by bus to get to work from his home south of the city.

Everywhere, a carnival for the eyes. We pass a makeshift clinic on the sidewalk—one man, one woman in gloves, two seats, one small table, a bottle of iodine, and a walkway of men lying on pavement, injecting themselves. Farther up the street: a man recycling syringes.

*****

I have earplugs in my ears and a scarf double-wrapped as tightly as can be around my head. The windows are shut, the fan and AC running full blast, and still the racket outside deafens me. Diwali, the festival of lights, is also a punishment of noise.

By the third night, I just want it over. The neighbors' speakers sit three floors below our window, on and off they go with no particular schedule, no concern for the sick and tired. At 2 a.m., the neighborhood guru prays and sings through the loudspeaker—a beautiful voice, but much too much too late. His two hours of chanting end at 4 a.m. with a welcome lull—but only until seven, when the music blares again.

On the final day of official festivities, we visit the river. Everywhere across Kolkata, neighbors and relatives band together to make likenesses of Kali, a multi-armed goddess with a string of human heads around her neck. She is known as the Dark Mother, the deity for whom this celebration is honored and for whom this city is named. Crowds of men carry and twirl her before the water, then lay her softly to rest in the gray, as orange sunlight swaddles her sinking, melting body.

Gongs and drums and noisemakers sound as truckloads arrive with giant statues at the center. Cops in helmets and berets stand guard with guns and batons as so many people come to the water, sending so many Kalis floating. Some are adorned in silk and gold, long hair and flowers. Some are painted neon blue, others the natural hues of terra-cotta and organic dyes. Her face generally floats a short while before finally dipping below the river's surface.

The refuse causes concern—so much Kali, so much paint, so many chemicals dumped straight into the waters that bathe, feed, and transport Kolkatans. In eras past, of course, the Dark Mother was made of natural materials. But today, Kali the Destroyer paints the river in toxic colors.

*****

It is Monday, the day after Diwali ends. Yet our neighbors still play the same repertoire of Bollywood music, a handful of thumping songs again and again and again. This block and only this block continues to romp. The rest of Kolkata slumbers in a bandh. A strike. The streets clear, shops shutter their doors. This is how India makes political protest. This bandh revolves around a place called Nandigram, where police allegedly killed fourteen villagers and wounded seventy more during protests against government plans to confiscate local lands for a special economic zone. In response, Nandigram allies have called for a citywide stop, a complete interruption of life. Only "necessary" businesses—including a scarce few tourist restaurants and shops, street food stalls, and tea wallahs—are allowed to remain open. Those who defy orders face scrutiny by the local mafia. Scrutiny is often conducted by a gang of men with clubs.

As I wander the vacant streets, young men walk beside me telling me of their "open market," asking, "Madame, do you need something? I think you must need something."

I ask the manager of Fresh & Juicy, a restaurant we frequent, about his business.

"Yes, yes, we are open."

27. Stuck in Kolkata - 2007

An oarsman ferries residents across Adi Ganga, a fetid branch of the Houghly River, between a residential area and Kalighat in Kolkata. Once the main course of the Houghly River, the Adi Ganga is now a grey-black sewage canal for much of southwest Kolkata, though it retains its holy history.

261

"It is not a problem for you?"

"No, not a problem, because I know somebody."

He sits outside on a plastic chair, beside the one open panel of his roll-down metal gates. All the rest are closed.

As are most across the city. Some shops remain open, but only just. Their gates are open a smidgen, their owners watch the street with cautious eyes. Some proprietors roll down their gates just enough to create an opening barely big enough to crawl beneath. Others have mini doors, little rectangles the size of cabinet doors, built right into the metal.

As Jerry leaves an open Internet shop, thugs with clubs approach on their motorcycles, speaking sternly to the manager. "There is no problem," the manager tells Jerry. "Well, there are some problems." But not with him because an Internet shop is considered an "essential" business.

It's a day of calm that doesn't feel calm.

*****

And just like that, the strike ends. A day early. Kolkata's commotion resumes.

We switch hotels, moving to a stately colonial-era relic called The Old Kenilworth, and we are suddenly in a different corner of the world. This place has stuck in the same Armenian family for half a century, closed and reopened, named and renamed through the years. It's a mansion with nine rooms and at least one huge dog to guard the home and gardens. Each room opens wide, with a cavernous bedroom, an adjoining sitting and drinking room overlooking the lawn, a spacious bathroom, and ceilings at least fifteen feet high. Our guidebook describes the rooms as "Spartan," but the description denies the charm and character that never exist in a new concrete block. It's got half a century of well-polished, well-scrubbed grime. I like it. It feels used; it feels full of stories.

We enter The Old Kenilworth doors to news of a cyclone headed our way. We have train tickets to Assam, but all reports indicate Tropical Storm Sidr will hit precisely the night and precisely the spot where we hope to cross northeastern India by train. It's a super cyclonic storm. Hunker down and batten down the hatches—so say the reports we read in the papers and online. Meteorologists predict this could be the century's biggest storm.

We change our tickets. We prepare for the worst—yet how does a traveler prepare for a cyclone? We ask the owner to tape our windows, but he has no tape; his demeanor is nonchalant.

We wander the city and nothing changes. People still amass as usual. They live and sleep and bathe on the street with no protection against the impending elements.

The night the cyclone is expected to hit, we dine at a vegetarian restaurant, reputed to be among the city's finest. But I can't savor my food. I have no stomach. I have only worries of the night to come. We return to our room and wait. A slight breeze rattles the trees. Lightning flickers through the sky. We curl in bed and, eventually, my eyes close and I sleep long hours.

We wake to a sunny morning, everything the same. Nothing. No storm, no shattered windows, no devastation—not here. Here, the sky is for the first time blue, swept clean by the storm's outlying winds. Just off the coast south of Kolkata, the cyclone turned east and pummeled Bangladesh instead, killing ten thousand people.

*****

On my first full day in Kolkata, I wake late after my middle-of-the-night arrival. I step into the miasma, walk two blocks from our hotel, and slice my toes on the sharp handle of a parked rickshaw. It doesn't hurt much, but I bleed on the street, and I attract a crowd. A nearby vendor offers me a stool and a young man races off to grab a crystal-like rock, which he carefully rubs across the injured toes. He holds my bleeding foot in his hand. He insists. A nearby woman chatters in Bengali and asks someone to translate, but no one does, or no one can. Yet I can tell, everyone is concerned that I treat the wound properly.

I am stunned. A stranger! Lifting my bloody foot, the dirtiest of all body parts, with his bare hands. It is a kindness that speaks to me above the noxious din of Kolkata.

It is a kindness that carries me through every indignity I see across India.

27. Stuck in Kolkata - 2007

A boy keeps an eye on things outside a string of closed shops during a "bandh" or strike, called by the Communist Party of India (Marxist) in West Bengal. These strikes, enforced with violence, bring the normally chaotic city to an unnerving, quiet standstill.

28. Finding Shu - 2010

I love and hate the knock. It almost always comes at first light, when the sky squints pink and my eyes clutch sleep. Tap tap tap. Growing louder, creeping closer as the conductor makes his way up the aisle and to our door. Tap tap. "Lao Cai! Lao Cai, Lao Cai, Lao Cai!" And then his voice trails, and so does the sound of knuckles against wood, in synch with the chug chug, chug chug, chug chug of the train.

We are here.

Shu's friend is here to collect us, along with eleven other foreigners and all of our bags. It's 5:30 a.m, and a gray sky hugs this cramped, damp town on the Chinese border. We pile into a van and angle up the road—two smooth, wide lanes of blacktop; a drainage ditch and barriers between us and the drop-off. Much has changed in eleven years. As we sweep upward over this mountain of terraced fields, we can see sections of the old pebbly road, long since overgrown. It looks like a footpath among the paddies.

We twist and turn with the pavement—I remember this. And the cloud, I remember the cloud. Partway up the mountain, the view slips into a veil of mist and we drive through obscurity. This I remember well.

We enter the outskirts of Sapa and make our way past so many hotels and pizza shops and cafes, and so many wide-eyed tourists engaging in the early morning. I don't remember a reservoir in the center of town. I don't remember this much town, really, which sprawls now in every possible direction.

But I remember Shu. There she is, in the street. The van stops outside the Pinocchio Hotel, and there is Shu—same face, same hair, same little girl I used to know now enveloped in a young woman's body. Jerry and I tumble from the van and into a frenzy of hugs and smiles. She has the same high-pitched voice, lodged deep inside the memory of my ears.

"Oh, it is very good to see you!" she says. "Did you think maybe we would never see each other again?"

I dreamed we would, someday. But I hadn't predicted e-mail. I hadn't imagined her as a woman; a mother; an entrepreneur with a business, a website, and a Facebook account. She tells me about the day she Googled herself. "I just search for my name and I found you—and my story," she says. "I think oh, who am I?" She read the story of a young Shu she did not entirely remember.

Shu shows us our room, a simple spot with a soft bed, hot water, and windows that open to a wide tile patio. But we cannot see anything from the veranda; the clouds let loose in a trickle of rain. There is no inkling of a mountain beyond, but it's there. This hotel sits in the precise location of the wooden home Shu shared with other Hmong women and girls when we first met. On this spot, eleven years ago, we bought a pair of jackets from a bag of embroideries stashed beneath Shu's bed.

After we shower and rest, Shu leads us to breakfast—our two arms linked as Jerry trails behind. We walk through a street in transformation. "I hate this," she says of the construction crews everywhere. So much growth draws so many people. But Shu prefers the foreigners of a previous age. "The tourists I met when I was young were better," she says. "Before they come because they love Vietnam. Now they come because they are just traveling."

She takes us to an all-you-can-eat brunch in the cozy dining room of a hotel where she formerly worked. She shoves a bowl of bright orange pumpkin soup my way, then a bowl of vegetarian pho and a plate of fruit, fried vegetables, and rice. She loads her own plate, takes a few spoonfuls of my soup, then goes for seconds. Ham and rice, she shovels it in. Her mouth is full and her words pour forth. She eats in gulps and thinks in volumes. Though her voice is the same, her language is all grown up.

"Maybe you can help me write my dream," she says.

She talks and talks and eats—she tells me so many things, I can't keep them all straight. She asks us questions about the Hmong in Laos and the Hmong in America. She thinks the Hmong in Laos are better educated and have more power than the Hmong in Vietnam. She wants to visit but says she cannot get a passport. She applied two years ago and paid fifteen dollars, but the government denied her application. "They did not give my fifteen dollars back. They said no." Just no; no explanation. "Because I am too good," she says in a low voice. She has done too much already. Shu is a force around town. She's savvy. In general, she says, she cannot trust the Vietnamese. Only some. Those "some" are the people she befriends. "Sometimes friend." This is precisely what she told me eleven years earlier.

I tell Shu she understands everything about life in Sapa, though she slightly disagrees. "Not everything—but some things. I live here. I should know some things."

When we return to the Pinocchio, she finds my website on her little netbook and brings up her story, our story. "That's me and you?" she asks, looking at a photo of the two of us walking.

"I thought you were very tall."

*****

We meet Shu's daughter, Ngoc Chau. She's almost five now, with short black hair and gigantic almond-shaped eyes. She is an energetic, smiley, much-younger pixie image of her mother. We see her just a few short minutes before she's scooped into the arms of a caretaker. Shu tells us she's a single mother. "Sometimes people are talking about that," she says. "But it's good. I am strong enough." She has lots of helpers to get Ngoc Chau through the day.

We spend that afternoon wandering the town, hand in hand or arm in arm. Shu leads us through the misty market, with a rainbow of garden goods below and handicrafts on the level above. In America, I say, the Hmong are known as farmers who sell some of the country's best fresh vegetables.

In Sapa, Shu says, no Hmong sell foods in the market. All the vendors are Vietnamese.

And with that, we slip back in time—back eleven years to the same conversations we had about hierarchy and social order. Shu has developed a philosophy through the years, and an adult's understanding of human nature. She figures, in general, of every hundred people on Earth, five are good. Those five live and work from the heart, she says. The rest do not. The rest can be jealous or lazy or they do bad things. She says this is true of all people, Hmong included. And she tells me she, too, has done bad things. I don't ask her what she means, I just tell her all humans err.

We stop by her mother's stall, where the petite woman is dwarfed by stacks of her own handiwork, in the most regal shades of blue and green. I immediately recall Cu's striking face, but she doesn't remember us. She apologizes, then unfurls a gorgeous bedspread that has captured our eyes. It takes Hmong women one year to complete a work such as this, Shu says, "because they also work in the fields." We buy the bedspread for the small price she asks—no haggling—and Cu insists we take a few trinkets as gifts.

Shu tells me her dreams—to buy a piece of land beside the main road where she could build a sturdy two-story structure for the Hmong in her home village. They could use that building as a market for selling their vegetables on one level and handicrafts on another. Now, she says, the Hmong have no place to work. A few, like her mother, sell embroideries in the main Sapa market, but most vendors there are Vietnamese. Many Hmong can't afford the rent. They have neither sufficient money nor education to start a business.

The Hmong own none of the businesses in Sapa. "It's all Vietnamese," she says. "One hundred percent." The Hmong have nothing to do. Even the timber we followed in 1999, when we searched for Hmong loggers working deep in the forest. "The wood is gone. Everything changes. It's all different." So the village women have no choice. They come to Sapa with baskets and bags of items to sell. They follow tourists through the streets, waving cloth before foreign eyes.

If the Hmong had a small building, Shu says, tourists could buy their souvenirs right in the village, where the money would stay. Her mind spins with ideas. The Hmong can't make money until they have education and training. For the past few years, Shu has been teaching village teenage girls to work as English- and French-speaking guides. A job means independence. It means freedom from marriage at sixteen, and options beyond the farm.

Shu dreams big. By her calculations, she's twenty-four years old. By mine, she's twenty-one or twenty-two. Either way, she says, too much of her life already has passed. She'd rather go back to the age she was when we met so she would have that many more years to dream, to learn, to work.

As we continue through town, we stop at the newly built tourist center, a beautiful colonial-style building with wide, rambling spaces for sitting, reading, and sipping tea. The walls are covered in photos, some of them depicting local kids with quotes about their thoughts on tourism. Shu points to a picture of her cousin, Ly Thi Mai, taken at the age of fourteen while standing on a boulder, clutching a pink bouquet of wildflowers. The girl said she wanted to have her portrait taken just as many tourists do, with a backdrop of terraced fields and deep valleys. She smiles in the picture. Two years ago, Shu says, Ly Thi Mai disappeared. Most likely, she was sold to someone in China, perhaps to be a wife, but no one knows for sure. That happens to Hmong girls in Sapa. One day they are your friends. One day, Shu says, they are gone.

*****

We wake to darkness. The sky pours forth. So we sit with Shu in the lobby of the Pinocchio Hotel, each of us with eyes on a separate computer screen, sending e-mails, reading news. Shu checks her Facebook page, her back hunched over a small table. Today, she wears a traditional Hmong outfit of hand-dyed indigo cotton. She tells me she likes the freedom to choose her clothes—some days she dresses Dao, other days Giay or Hmong. With indigo across her skin, fingers on her phone, and eyes intent on her little netbook screen, Shu is the picture of modernity and change.

By noon, the rain lifts and tendrils of stringy white clouds shoot up the valleys, tangling with higher clouds coming down, as though two layers of fingers interlace across a wall of mountains. This is our guesthouse view. Across the street is a bar selling cocktails and a restaurant with pizza and steak.

We head for lunch to Shu's favorite restaurant, the Tam Xuyen, and order an array of dishes to share: pork with mushroom, water spinach with garlic, fried chicken and bamboo. We eat while Shu tells stories; this is our ritual. She does not want to marry a Hmong man from Sapa because she thinks many men don't like to work hard. And she doesn't want to marry an old man, not a man her father's age. That happens frequently in Asia but "I don't think it's a good life."

Maybe she will go to Laos to marry. Maybe the Hmong life is better there. Many Hmong girls marry tourists, she says, but not for the reasons people might think. "Hmong don't marry for money," she says. "They marry for love…love is important, you think?" She thinks so.

Shu says her parents are "too good." Her mother never raises her voice; her father shares his money until he has none left to give. "I don't know why my family is like this." I understand what she means. She appreciates their generosity, but she has seen too many of her people wilt in the winds of greed and poverty. They don't often say no. They give and give until the wind leaves them hobbled in its wake. Strength means everything to Shu. It's the hope she has.

After we've eaten, we walk the rocky trail—again—to Cat Cat. I'd forgotten how beautiful and steep this valley is. Shu hands me her cell phone and asks if I'll carry it in my purse. "If I put it in my bag it will be all blue," she says. Indigo dye. A few moments later, the phone rings. Shu takes it, answers, then hands the phone to me again. "OK, you are my porter."

A few tourists hike ahead of us. Men on motos ride toward us, up the steep grade of the mountainside. They ask if we'd like a seat on their bikes—but no, we walk. Shu tells us the government has sold all the land lining the road near the ticket house (foreigners pay 20,000 dong to visit the village) so that private companies now run cafes and galleries along the way. We reach the cobbled path heading through the village. Even here, Shu says, the Vietnamese, not the Hmong, own the trinket shops.

She takes us into a thatch-and-wood home of an old woman who sells embroidered purses—some her own, others she has bought. About fifteen people live in this small, dim house, Shu says. The woman has a passel of kids; they all married and now have their own.

Two young boys watch a Hmong show on TV, broadcast from Thailand. This is usual, Shu says. It's a problem. Too many Hmong kids spend their days watching TV. Some go to school, but they don't learn much. And instruction is all in Vietnamese.

Suddenly, a Vietnamese woman with a microphone and a man with a video camera enter the home. They're filming a TV show and want us to be in it—but we decline. Jerry and I explain to Shu the complications of us getting into the public eye when we're here to ask questions of others. The government, as she knows well, doesn't like that.

Farther down the path, across the roiling waters that crash over boulders and swamp the valley with noise, we meet another friend of Shu's. The woman says her husband has taken two additional wives, and she's not happy. She has six kids of her own, and the family can't afford to feed so many mouths. She and her husband routinely fight. Shu chats with her in Hmong for quite some time as Jerry and I admire the waters. I tell Shu she's like a counselor to her neighbors and friends.

She tells me the story of another friend, a young woman whose parents pressured her to marry. But Shu told her if she did, she would work in the field and life would continue for generations more as it has for centuries already. So the girl stayed single and told Shu she is happy working in Sapa making her own money, saving her own money.

By contrast, Shu has another friend who married a man from Cat Cat and moved to the village to be with him. That young woman now has three children and a handful of problems. Shu says marriage is like the umbilical cord to family, culture, and village. But she wants something different. Shu has advice for any young woman: save your own money and pursue a new way.

She has an idea. She wants the two of us to write a book about the Hmong of Sapa. She will take a questionnaire to the villagers each time she goes trekking. She will ask questions about people's lives and their histories, and she will record their answers. I will help her write the book. Jerry will fill it with photos. And the book will help teach people—tourists, the Vietnamese, even the Hmong— about Hmong culture. The profits will help build a school and establish a fund for needy Hmong women. And if the government doesn't like that idea, Shu says, so be it. The book can be printed elsewhere, and the Hmong in America can buy the book and send it to their relatives in Vietnam.

*****

Shu's mind is always working this way. She takes me to the top floor of the Pinocchio, where she plans to knock down a wall and create a space for training guides. She will build a small bar where tourists can drink and watch the stars. And she will remodel the kitchen in preparation for cooking classes. Shu loves

Author Karen Coates walks through a local market with Shu, a young Hmong woman who works as a tour guide and small-scale local entrepreneur helping other young Hmong women out of the usual cycle of child bearing and poverty.

to cook, and she promises a feast for us.

It's late afternoon and the sky dims above a light rain. Together, we meander the cramped corridors of the Sapa market. Shu noses her way through piles of greens, roots, and chiles. She plucks an armload of lime green "cat cabbage" with spiky, oaklike leaves, then selects the freshest scallions, tomatoes, and tofu. She angles next toward a table laden with freshly butchered pork. After inspecting each piece, she selects a thick, pink slab of clean meat.

The rain stops by the time we reach the hotel, and Shu sets to work on cleaning the greens, removing their roots. She places her tiny wooden stool on the veranda's burnt-orange tiles, still slick from the afternoon showers. Big, billowy clouds flirt with the mountaintop across the way.

The kitchen is just a few steps from the porch, and a couple of Shu's trainees are here for their evening work. This hotel provides more than a job for a dozen or so youngsters. It's a place to eat and sleep, a respite far from their village homes scattered throughout these hills. Every night, every employee gathers for a family-style meal, served on one big table. It is Hmong custom. No one eats alone. Everyone is family. And we are included in the invitation.

"In your country, you have tofu?" Shu asks.

Yes, I say, but it's not as good and not as varied.

"OK, I show you how to cook tofu."

She lights a gas burner and pours vegetable oil into a wok. Then she grips the long, rectangular block of tofu in one hand and slices it into cubes, sliding them into the bubbling oil. Plop, sizzle. Each piece, fried until golden brown, perfectly maintains its shape. "You know, I usually cook a lot for my tourists," Shu says. She removes the tofu and lets it cool while she chops tomatoes and scallions.

Meanwhile, in the back corner, a young woman stuffs the pork slab into a blender—instant pork puree, to be mixed with scallions, rolled into wild betel leaves, and fried until fragrant.

"OK, we go," Shu says suddenly, unexpectedly. There is much more to prepare, but she has other plans. Her life is a constant buzz of duties. A California filmmaker is here to interview Shu about her culture, the Hmong, and the recent unsettling trend of disappearing hilltribe girls. By the time we return to the kitchen, an hour or so later, the greens have been fried and the tofu sits in its ruddy stew.

But it's not yet time to eat. An hour of relaxation is upon us. We watch a spectacular dance of clouds across the mountains until the sun droops and the night grows black. The staff then lounges through a TV show until finally it is time. We are all called to the table. Dishes of tofu and betel-wrapped spring rolls sit among a tureen of broth with medicinal herbs; a platter of fish wrapped in pickled leaves; a plate of garlic with fried greens; and the cat cabbage, which tastes deeply bitter. It evokes memories of my grad school days in Hanoi, fourteen years earlier, when I ate that cabbage almost every day. Shu says it's consumed for good health, as most bitter vegetables are.

We fill our bowls with plump, nutty grains of mountain rice, and we serve each other bits and bobs from the array before us. We eat until we can eat no more. Then the women leave to relax in their rooms while the men linger around tiny cups of hot green tea, then cups of cold rice whiskey. We admire the foggy night, and the colorful, shadowy light on the streets below.

*****

The next morning, the Pinocchio lobby is a bustle of activity. Shu has asked me to take notes as her girls—young guides in training tell me about their lives. She wants me to record their dreams, and she wants Jerry to take their photos, so she can post their biographies online as an introduction to their customers.

There is Lo Thi Mao, sixteen, from Lao Chai village. She became a tourist guide in order to help her family. She dreams of speaking English fluently—and, one day, traveling to Australia or Canada. Chiang Thi Chi, seventeen, is teaching herself French because Sapa does not have many French-speaking guides. She comes from Ta Van village, where her parents live with her seven brothers and three sisters. Lo Thi Lang, at eighteen, is the eldest of nine kids. She dreams of speaking fluent English so she can support her family back on the farm. Lo Thi So is almost seventeen. She grew up among the rice fields of Lao Chai. Now, she stays in Sapa and sends her earnings back home. She hopes someday to earn enough money and save a little bit for herself. Her dream is to travel around Vietnam.

The young women all wear hand-dyed indigo outfits they sewed for themselves. They gather with Shu before a red brick wall, smiling for the camera. And then we're off.

With Cliff, the filmmaker, we all pile onto mopeds to tackle the serpentine road east through an emerald world. Our aim is Hau Thao village, to meet a woman named Sao, whose twenty-six-year-old daughter, Peng, disappeared a few months before.

Everyone in the village knows. Everyone believes she was "sold to China," just as her sister had been a year earlier. And everyone says it happens when unmarried—or divorced, in Peng's case—women mingle with "bad boys": young Hmong men who befriend young Hmong girls and then send them across the border into China. It's good money for the men. It feeds a lot of local drug and gambling habits.

We park our motos at a small shop along the highway and climb the steep, rocky path to Hau Thao. Sao meets us at the foot of her home, and we all squat in a conversation. I ask Sao if she has talked to the police about her daughter, but she has not. She tells us she has no education and she does not know how to ask for help. So she keeps on living, each day like the next, in her wooden home on a mud-packed floor at the base of a striking vertical green mountain. And when tourists—not many, but some—come through Hau Thao, she sells her embroidered purses and pillowcases for a few dollars.

Cliff knew Peng. Nine years earlier, he and his wife met the girl when she was working as a tourist guide. "We wondered all these years what happened to Peng," he says.

"She was a good tourist guide," Sao says. "Then she got married." Two and a half years later, she divorced her opium-smoking husband and returned to work in Sapa, taking her young daughter with her. A man she knew asked her to travel to Lao Cai for work. The women here suspect he promised Peng good things— that's what typically happens. Peng left her daughter with a friend and went to Lao Cai. After two days, the friend wondered why Peng hadn't returned. After three days, Sao traveled to Sapa and retrieved her granddaughter from the babysitting friend. No one has seen Peng since.

"She's been gone about four and a half months already," Sao says. She has lived this story twice. She explains that Peng's younger sister disappeared when she was twenty-one or twenty-two years old (the Hmong aren't always exact with ages). Her friends suspect she followed her boyfriend out of town and onto a track that led her to China. One year gone, and she has not returned.

"I don't know if my daughters are still alive or dead," Sao says, "so I don't know if I will see them again." Peng's 3½-year-old daughter clings to her grandmother throughout the interview.

Locals say the disappearances started three or four years earlier. In this village: the two sisters. Another village up the road: six or seven girls. "It happens every year," Shu says. The village chiefs do nothing, and neither do the police.

Power. That is what Shu most wants for her girls. It is the thing she says they do not have. She thinks they will gain it only through education.

*****

We chat a little while longer, then return to our motorcycles for a quick trip west to Ta Van. Shu is opening a homestay in this village, and she wants Jerry to take pictures. Ads, really. For her website. It's a sparkling new concrete structure with a wooden upper floor. A spacious porch overlooks the vast green valley and, beyond that, a wall of mountains. Shu is going to charge three dollars a night for a mattress on the wooden floor with mosquito net dangling from above. For ten dollars, guests can get a few home-cooked meals. The house has an indoor toilet and a hot water shower. "Simple," Shu says. "Very simple." She hopes to hire two or three village women who otherwise have no work.

Next stop: Lao Chai, the village where Shu grew up. It's just down the road and over a few miles of pebbled earth. We head that way on our motorcycles, meeting lines of tourists hiking in our direction. This is new. When Shu first took us home to her mother and father, in 1999, we were the only foreigners in sight. The road is still terrible.

I barely recognize the village. But Shu reminds me time and again: this prosperity does not belong to the Hmong. Most every tourist dollar goes to the Vietnamese.

Except her business—a nonprofit marked by a large sign denoting Sapa O'Chau as "the FIRST H'mong owned and run trekking business and home stay in Sapa." Of this, Shu is proud. The A-frame metal roof covers an upstairs sleeping room with a similar setup to that in Ta Van. On the ground floor is a breezy dining room with open walls.

Shu encourages us to try the house specialty, advertised on the sign out front. "Get hip with organic hemp milk. Most nutritious food available." The plants surround the home. Shu says the milk comes from crushing the seeds. Though it's Cannabis sativa, it won't make you high. "Not the same," Shu says.

In the next room over, an assemblage of uncles and a thin, gray grandfather eat their lunch while delving into a bottle of rice wine. "Happy water," Shu calls it. Except she doesn't really think it's happy when Hmong men stay inside, drinking and gambling, while the women huff their way into town in order to sell their wares, or work in the kitchen to feed tourists.

Cliff, the filmmaker, looks around and asks Shu whether villagers make money from their fields, growing rice to sell.

"No," she says unequivocally. The Hmong have never had a monetized economy. Villagers feed their families with the rice and corn they grow. When Cliff asks what, then, the people can sell, she says: handicrafts.

We escape the heat and sit to a meal of rice, fried tofu with tomato, and fried green beans that grow among the cannabis beside the house. It's delicious. Shu is ravenous; she was too busy in the morning to eat her breakfast, and now she inhales—again, just as I remember her, eleven years before.

All the while, tourists plod the trail uphill as barefoot men plow the muddy earth with the bulk of their water buffalo. It's planting season. It is the cyclical life Shu and her people know.

The tourists all come from Sapa. They come with guides, and they all trek the same loop. They pass right by Shu's big sign, and this bucolic dining room among the fields that grow our food.

This book? A book of the Hmong? Shu tells me she doesn't care how long it takes, she doesn't care if she earns no money. (Though a little money would help—she could put it into a bank account and maybe, one day, that money would grow and she could build a house for single mothers.)

That's Shu's dream—for the book, for life. "It's OK," she says, as she often does. She believes in the future, she believes in one day. "I don't care if it takes five or six years," she says.

Her dreams have no deadlines.

*****

Late that afternoon, the sun streams through intermittent clouds as we prepare to leave Sapa. I sit with Shu in the hotel lobby, her "office," and we talk about mundane things. There is always meaning in mundane chitchat when it's the last conversation with a good friend you won't see for a while.

And then it's time. Shu walks us to the street, where we pile into a crowded van with half a dozen tourists and an enormous lot of stuff. Shu and I hold hands until I'm in my seat and she's in the street, waving, smiling. We bounce on down the winding road and I peer across deep valleys carved with fields of rice.

We arrive at the train station more than an hour before our departure, so we sit outside at a boisterous restaurant and we fill our bellies with noodles. The street noise feels jarring after the past few days of mountain quiet.

That night, we share a cabin with a couple of Swedish women on holiday. They read paperbacks and I write in my journal as the train clunk-clunk clunk-clunk clunk-clunks down the tracks, through the darkness, toward Hanoi. We arrive before dawn, before the place has shed its shroud of damp evening air. Within an hour we are checking in at the airport; within a few more hours, we are back in Bangkok in the center of political riots and a city in flames. Twenty hours and 650 miles from Sapa.

I have this image of Shu in my head: She wears her indigo clothes as we stand on a bridge with a rushing stream beneath us. She's smiling. The air smells sweet. And when it's time to go, she reaches out to hold my hand. Together we go walking.

*Jerry Redfern and
Karen Coates in Laos.*

Afterword

And that's it. It's not the end of the story, the end of Shu, or the end of our story together. Nor is it the end of my travels. But it's all I have of Shu in my journal. Jerry and I get on a bus and then a train and then a plane, and we go home. And there my writing ceases for a while.

It's a funny thing—I try to keep a journal at home in the United States. It never works (though I will always keep trying). I set goals for myself; every morning or every evening at sunset, I'll write about the birds and the trees and the garden that gives us tomatoes. I'll write about the little lizards that skitter across our yard, and the big picnic table where we eat summertime barbecues beneath our mulberry tree. I'll write a page one day, a paragraph the next, then nothing. It simply doesn't work. Yet when I am traveling, I never forgo my journal. A day or two without is like not eating, not drinking; a week, and I've given up breath.

At home, it's different. I take notes for articles; I don't linger over a pot of tea with a leather-bound journal in hand.

It's not that I don't like our home in the Rio Grande Valley with some of the world's greatest sunsets and a sky that knows every crayon in the box. I love it. But I also have to move. I have to be out of place to feel at home in my words.

And I have to be at home in my words to really know who I am.

Acknowledgments

I dedicate these stories to the countless people I have encountered on roads and trails, at work and at play, in kitchens and in fields across Asia. Some of you are named within these pages, others of you are here in spirit. All of you have transformed my life and made me who I am today. I hope, in some small way, I have offered you something along the way. Thank you for the memories and lessons learned.

Thank you, Janet, for your unfailing support, encouragement, and understanding—even as the months continued to pass and still, no finished manuscript had made its way to your inbox. Until now. You are a writer's dream editor. Thank you for making these stories into a book.

And thank you, Jerry, for a life of companionship and love. Every morning, when the earnest robin sings or the blasted rooster crows, I begin a new journey with you.

Karen J. Coates

"I've been hooked on Asia ever since I spent a semester of graduate school in Hanoi more than a dozen years ago. Somehow I managed to wheedle my husband, photojournalist Jerry Redfern, into a life on the move. I took a newspaper job in Phnom Penh in 1998, shortly after we married, and we've been tromping through jungles and rice paddies ever since. I spent a year studying food security and climate-change issues on a Ted Scripps Fellowship in Environmental Journalism at the University of Colorado. I'm a Southeast Asia correspondent for Archaeology, and I write a Food Culture column for The Faster Times. My work appears around the world, in publications including GlobalPost, Wall Street Journal Asia, Travel + Leisure Southeast Asia, National Geographic Books, Fodor's Travel Guides and many others. You can get a taste of my writing on my food blog, Rambling Spoon."

Jerry Redfern

Jerry Redfern began his career as a staff photographer at newspapers in the American West, at a time when papers still had darkrooms and photographers still processed their own film. In 1998, he and Karen moved to Cambodia where he shot news, features and investigative stories for Agence France-Presse, The New York Times, The Cambodia Daily and other publications. Redfern's work has won awards from numerous journalism and art organizations, including the Fund for Investigative Journalism, Center – Review Santa Fe, and the National Press Photographers Association. Redfern's images appear in publications around the world, including Natural History, The Wall Street Journal, Forbes, Archaeology, Travel+Leisure Southeast Asia, GEO, Sierra, National Geographic Books, and many others.